S0-FKH-203

PAINTERS AT THE SIKH COURT

SCHRIFTENREIHE DES SÜDASIEN-INSTITUTS
DER
UNIVERSITÄT HEIDELBERG

BAND 20

FRANZ STEINER VERLAG GMBH · WIESBADEN
1975

PAINTERS AT THE SIKH COURT

A STUDY
BASED ON TWENTY DOCUMENTS

BY

BRIJINDER NATH GOSWAMY

FRANZ STEINER VERLAG GMBH · WIESBADEN
1975

CIP-Kurztitelaufnahme der Deutschen Bibliothek

Painters at the Sikh Court: a study based on twenty documents.
(Schriftenreihe des Südasien-Instituts der Universität Heidelberg; Bd. 20)

ISBN 3-515-02097-7
NE: Goswamy, Bigendra N. [Hrsg.]

 Satz und Druck: Druckerei Wolf, Heppenheim
Printed in Germany

"Lovers in a Forest"

Painting in the 'Kangra' Style done
for a Sikh Patron in the Punjab Plains.
I quarter of the XIX century.
(Courtesy: National Museum, N.Delhi)

PREFACE

This is a book which offers only a part of what its title promises. This study does not cover either the whole body of painters active in the Punjab Plains in the XIX cent., or all that happened at the Sikh Court in the matter of patronage of the arts. The core of the work consists of a group of twenty documents: fifteen of them in Persian, and relating to grants of land to a family of Pahari painters working for Sikh patrons; four of them in Urdu, from the period immediately following the British occupation of the Kangra Hills; and one of them in Hindi, being a petition possibly to the Maharani of Chamba. What ties this group of documents together is the fact that they all come from one family collection, which I had the good fortune to chance upon, and the fact that they relate to a short but active period of history and to a family of artists that is significant to the history of Indian Painting. If, then, there is in these pages no history of painting in the Punjab, there is at least the flavour of the period. These documents concern themselves with facts and provide the structure of information upon which our study of painting in the Punjab can be based.

This publication is based upon the conviction that the study of material like this is not only relevant, but significant. We have yet to learn a great deal of how things happened behind the scenes, how painters and patrons came together, what precise relationships were worked out, and what the social and the economic situation of the artist in India of the past was. Hopefully, these documents will make a contribution of some kind to our understanding of the past. One only wishes that from other periods of Indian art, and other schools, comparable information had been accessible. We might then have been able to fill some of the silences in our dialogue with the past.

The pattern adopted for the presentation of this material follows that of the two earlier studies of historical documents, *The Mughals and the Jogis of Jakhbar*, and the *Mughal and Sikh Rulers and the Vaishnavas of Pindori*, that I published together with Professor J.S. Grewal some years ago. A detailed introduction setting the material in its historical and socio-economic-administrative context precedes the section in which the documents are presented. At the risk of appearing pedantic, not only the facsimiles and the translations have been included, but also transcriptions in *nastaliq* characters and, hopefully useful, notes. The *shikasteh* of the original presents serious difficulties of reading and the transcriptions have been included to provide scholars with some assistance in playing at the game of decipherment with these texts, should they be so inclined. The notes have aimed at providing relevant detail and if either they or some of the documents themselves seem somewhat repetitive, a possible justification for their inclusion lies in our awareness that each scholar addresses his own set of questions to material such as this.

This work has been possible only with the help which I have been privileged to receive from friends and scholars. The foremost of my debts is to Sri Chandu Lal, descendant of the family of artists to which these documents relate, for it is through his courtesy and that of his family that I was able to obtain these papers. In the matter of translation and interpretation of these documents, I have received consistent help from Professor J.S. Grewal, Mr. V.S. Suri and Mr. K.C. Grover. Sardar Ram Kumar of Haridwar and Pandit Haribilas of Kurukshetra gave me kind permission to consult their records and in the preparation of this manuscript I have received consideration and assistance from many persons: my wife, Karuna Goswamy, Mr. Hargopal Jhamb. Mr. Darwesh, Dr. Anna L. Dahmen-Dallapiccola, Miss Jutta Neubauer and Dr. Jürgen Lütt. The brevity with which I am aknowledging these kindnesses bears, I am aware, little or no relationship to the generous measure of help that I have received.

Finally, it was as a Jawaharlal Nehru Fellow for 1969 and 197o that I was able to collect most of the material presented in this book, and I would like to take this opportunity to thank the authorities of the Jawaharlal Nehru Memorial Fund not only for the grant of the Fellowship which enabled me to do this work but for their consistent generosity of attitude throughout its tenure.

Heidelberg, July 1o, 1974 B.N.G.

CONTENTS

INTRODUCTION

I. The Find

Not far from the main road that connects Pathankot in the Punjab with Kangra, now in Himachal Pradesh, a little over a mile on foot from the wayside village of Ladwara, is the picturesque hamlet of Gaggal.[1] Here, in a grove of stately, shady trees and surrounded by boulders with a rippling little stream of water flowing through them, is a small group of neat, typically modest Pahari houses. In one of these lives the painter Chandu Lal Raina, descendant of the great Nainsukh whose name is a legend among historians of Pahari painting.[2]

I have had occasion to visit the homes of Chandu Lal and his collaterals several times, talking to the painter and his family and making my notes.[3] In these visits I have seen vignettes of life as it must have been lived by his ancestors generations ago: a vaidya or physician looking in to examine a sick person and then staying on for hours, just conversing; a dom and his women arriving early in the morning with their clarinette and drums, singing songs that announce the beginning of a new desi month and collecting their traditional dues in the form of flour and dal and a few coins. And I have often had surprises of a pleasant kind, for the amount of oral information to be gathered from the family seems endless and there is always something to be added to what I had recorded in my last visit. During one of these visits, in 1968, in my effort to go through all that the painter's family had by way of records, visual or written, I chanced upon an old bamboo-tube on a high shelf.[4] No one knew or cared about what it contained: it was just a hollow, old bamboo-tube. I was, however, curious. With some persistence I managed to peer inside and take out a roll of old papers loosely wrapped in a pink silken cloth and very lightly tied with a string. All but one of the documents were in Persian[5] and no one in the family knew what they were about. Even after I unrolled them and spread them out and asked, no one could give me a clue to their contents. Chandu Lal who himself reads and writes Urdu fluently, could not make anything of them with certainty. From having worked with similar documents before, however, I was able to see even in a glance that these were records of grants that had been issued in favour of Chandu Lal's ancestors by the Sikh Sardars and princes at Lahore in the 19th century.

It took me long and arduous hours to decipher the shikasteh of their scipts which tended to become more and more unnegotiable as the size of the document became smaller.[6] Some of the words still remained problematic, but there was very little doubt about the general content of these papers. They were not original, detailed grants of the category of the farmans[7] and pattas[8] which we sometimes find in the course of fieldwork; they were mostly parwanas[9] containing follow-up action on the original grants now lost; there were gaps of unaccounted time between them if one arranged them in a chronological sequence. But they contained dates; names of painters, patrons, functionaries; even terms upon which the painters were engaged. Taken together, they were clearly important, for they represented, as far as I am aware, the only body of evidence of its kind in the whole range of Indian art history.[10] These documents added much to our information on Sikh patronage of painting, and told us a great deal of the situation of the Pahari painters of the 19th century; but they also did more than that: they contributed to our total understanding of the relationship of painter to patron as it obtained in India in the past.

It is this group of documents which is presented in the pages that follow.

II. The Painters

The "musavvirs" or painters who find direct mention in these documents: Nikka, his three sons Harkhu, Gokal and Chhajju, Damodar, son of Gokal, and Saudagar son of Chhajju, all belong to the family that is known to art historians as 'the family of Pandit Seu'. This is perhaps the most gifted of the families of Pahari artists on which we have at present any factual evidence of significance. Much on the history of this family has been published.[11] and a bare summary of it here will suffice. The style of this group of artists has also received detailed treatment at the hands of several scholars.[12] In some ways, it is a family the members of which, both past and present, have perhaps been on the best of terms with historians of Pahari art.

The genealogical tree of the family, as at present known, takes us back to Data, great grandfather of Seu,[13] into the 17th century, but the family still remains known as the family of Pandit Seu, for we do not know of the earlier work of its members, and Seu, one of whose portraits has survived,[14] was the one to whom our knowledge went back, when the family started being written about. Seu had two sons, the elder Manaku and the younger, Nainsukh. Both of these again are known to us as much from their portraits[15] which are available as from their work which has gained for their style a decided measure of respect. Manaku had two sons, Fattu and Khushala, whom we know something of also; Nainsukh had four sons: Kama, Gaudhu, Nikka and Ranjha. We have portraits of all four of them, and a great deal of work which is ascribable to their generation in this family.[16]

At one time, it was widely believed that this was a family of immigrant artists trained in the Mughal manner of painting of the Muhammad Shah period which had chosen to escape to the hills from the chaos of the plains in the second quarter of the 18th century, and made them its home. It was also speculated that they were Kashmiri Brahmins who had become attached to the court of some Pahari ruler or the other who settled them in the hills. The view that it is now possible to take, on the strength of inscriptional and oral evidence, is that the family belonged to the hills themselves and originated from Guler.[17] As early as A.D. 1736 we find Manaku making a pilgrimage to Haridwar from his native Guler, writing his name down in the registers of his family priests there in his own hand in the script of the hills, Takri, and mentioning his profession as that of 'Carpenter-painters'. Nainsukh also follows Manaku to Haridwar some years later and makes his own and detailed entry in A.D. 1763 in the register of the family priests, once again leaving little doubt that the family treated of Guler as their native place and described their profession as that of 'Carpenter-painters', notwithstanding the Brahmin appellation of 'Pandit' before the names of Seu, Manaku and Nainsukh in the inscriptions on their portraits. Quite obviously, as the family grew, especially in the generation after that of Nainsukh, the small but cultured state of Guler was unable to absorb and use all the talent that it had. Younger members of the family went and settled in other states, seeking fresh patronage and founding branches of their own of what might be called the 'family style'. Nainsukh himself had served a Jasrota prince, Balwant Singh, who inspired some of his most wonderfully warm and intimate studies of men and their moods;[18] he later settled in Basohli, serving its pious ruler, Amrit Pal, till his own death in 1778. His youngest son, Ranjha, had also made Basohli his home. We do not know much about Kama: perhaps he continued to live in Guler till his early death. Gaudhu apparently served Maharaja Sansar Chand of Kangra, that great patron of painting in the hills, if the indirect reference to Gaudhu in a fascinating letter written to Sansar Chand by the painter Shiba is any indication.[19] Nikka, the third of the sons of Nainsukh, and the first to find mention in our documents here, came and settled at Gaggal in the _mauza_ of Rajol in the fertile _taaluqa_ of Rihlu which was then part of the domains of Raja Raj Singh of Chamba.[20] Our knowledge of Nikka's move from Guler to Rajol, to the very piece of land on which the family home stands today, is based both on oral evidence available in the family and on the British Land Settlement records of A.D. 1868 which refer to Nikka "having settled on this piece of land measuring 32 _kanals_ with the permission of the then ruler". The British records do not mention a _patta_ or grant citing the conferment of this land, but the family tradition insistently recalls that there was a silver-plate which recorded the original grant, presumably given by Raja Raj Singh to Nikka.[21] The exact date of Nikka's migration is not known, but it must have taken place some time between A.D. 1764, the year of Raj Singh's accession and 1794, the year in which he died fighting for the retention of the rich lands of Rihlu against the more ambitious and intrepid Sansar Chand of Kangra.

The members of the Seu-Manaku-Nainsukh family worked in and took their style to a far greater number of states in the hills and outside than have been connected with them above. It is almost as if making Guler, Basohli and Rajol as their base, they fanned out over considerable stretches of territory. A visual representation of the spread of the members of this family, carrying their style with them, is to be found in a remarkable drawing showing a Devi with numerous arms. This 'magic diagram' as we can call it, points to the members of this family having served the rulers and princes of as many as nineteen different states, large and small, in the hills.[22] Among the patrons served by this family are also three Sikh Chiefs, mentioned by name: Jai Singh Kanhaiya,[23] his son Gurbakhsh Singh,[24] and Jassa Singh Ramgarhia.[25] It is this last piece of information in the diagram which is perhaps the most relevant to the present documents, for here we have an early reference to painters serving Sikh chiefs as early as in the 18th century.

The names of the individual artists who served in these various centres and the different chiefs are not given in the diagram, but we do have fairly complete information about the genealogy of this family from the point of the generation of Nikka onwards. This is how the family tree runs, coming down to Chandulal:

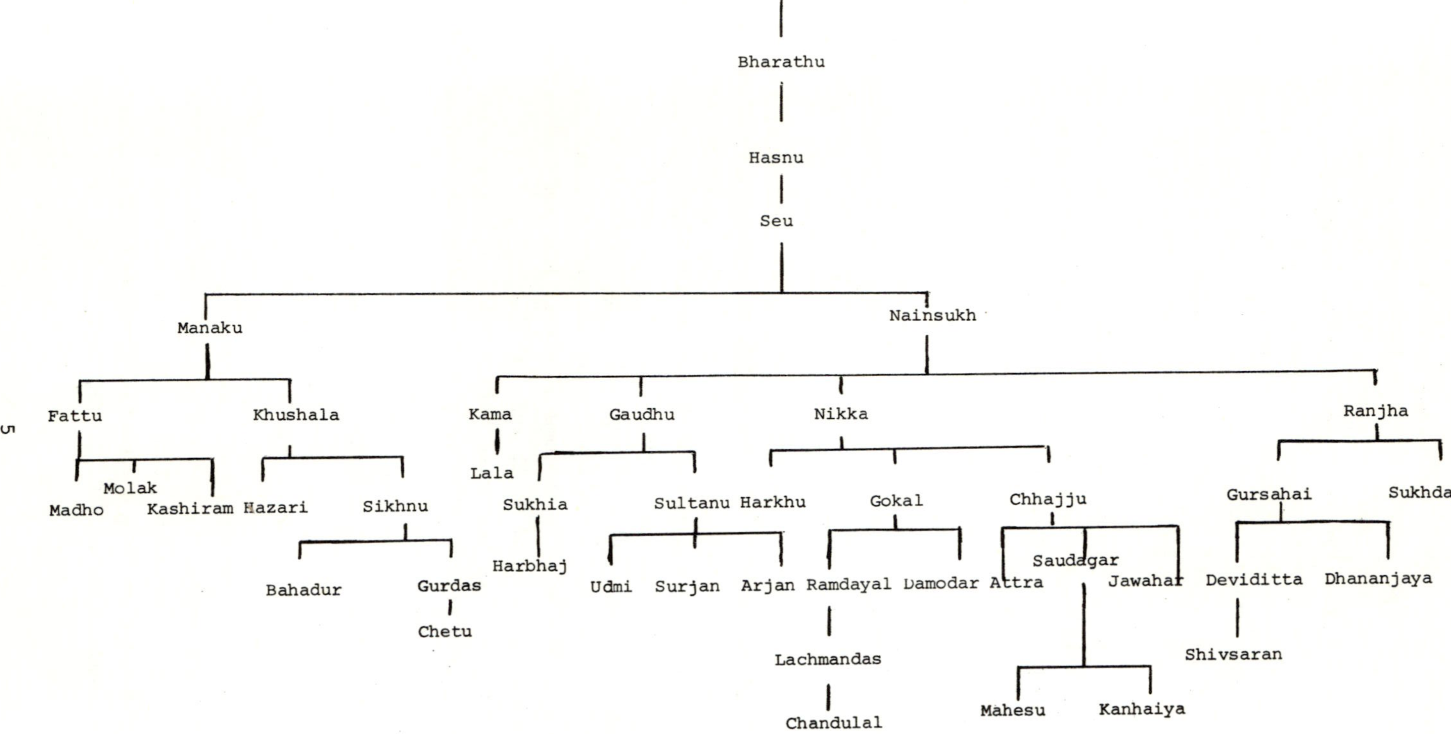

Data
Bharathu
Hasnu
Seu
Manaku
Nainsukh
Fattu
Khushala
Kama
Gaudhu
Nikka
Ranjha
Molak
Madho
Kashiram
Hazari
Sikhnu
Lala
Sukhia
Sultanu
Harkhu
Gokal
Chhajju
Gursahai
Sukhdayal
Saudagar
Bahadur
Gurdas
Harbhaj
Udmi
Surjan
Arjan
Ramdayal
Damodar
Attra
Jawahar
Deviditta
Dhananjaya
Chetu
Lachmandas
Shivsaran
Mahesu
Kanhaiya
Chandulal

The records from the hills are not over-abundant, but we can piece together information on some of the dates of the six painters who find mention in these documents from the registers of the priests at centres of pilgrimage visited by members of this family and from the successive Settlement records of the years 1868 and 1892.[26] It appears that Nikka lived to a ripe old age, dying in c.A.D. 1833, the year in which his ashes were taken for immersion into the Ganges at Haridwar.[27] Harkhu died childless in about 185o; Gokal who had two sons, Damodar and Ramdayal, died in about 1847; and Chhajju who had three sons, Attra, Saudagar and Jawahar, died in about 185o. Damodar and Saudagar, the remaining two painters who find mention here, were apparently alive in A.D. 1847, the year to which the last of our documents here belongs.

If the family of Pandit Seu finds frequent mention in art history, it is for other reasons than the fact that at present more is known about it from documentary sources than about other families of artists in the hills. It is chiefly for its style that the family receives recognition and respect from art historians and collectors alike. This style, for the most part, is the style that is roughly designated in its earlier phase as 'Guler' and in its later phase as 'Kangra'.[28] It is a style of incredible refinement and delicacy, full of poetry and warmth and a flowing but reticent grace. It is in this style that some of the great sets of 'Kangra' paintings have been rendered; and it is the leaves of the well-known Bhagavata-Purana, the Gita Govinda, the Satsai, the Ragamala and the Nala-Damayanti sets that best define and establish the characteristics of the style from the point of Nainsukh onwards. It all begins in a sense with Manaku and Nainsukh who experimented and evolved a style which grew out of a fusion of the bold and energetic style of 'Basohli' with the softer and more romantic style that belonged to the early 18th century at the Mughal Court. But once formed, the style continued with some amendment and some hardening, to the generation of Harkhu and Gokal and Chhajju.

The documents that are presented here contain no information on the style of the artists to whom they relate. They make not even an oblique reference to their work: but this is no great loss, for we do know that style very well already. They are significant for other things that they tell us of, for we know so little about them at present.

III. The Patrons

The present group of documents will serve, hopefully, as a significant source of information for the patronage of painting by the Sikhs, an activity which has received little attention and some scorn.[29] We have tended generally to take a somewhat dim view of the artistic interests of the Sikhs who, as W.G. Archer says,[3o] have been taken in this matter to be "humble products of the Punjab Plains, newcomers to Indian culture and, in origin, rough and simple peasants". Mr. Archer's brilliant work on Sikh Painting succeeds in correcting, as indeed it sets out to do, this impression. His work seems sharply to point out that the paintings of the Sikhs can no longer be treated as unimportant or irrelevant to the history of Indian painting; the developments in painting at Lahore and other centres of power and patronage in the Punjab were clearly important, and need to be studied in detail.

In doing this, Mr. Archer explores with great ability and at considerable length, first, the political developments of the period and the situation in the hills in the early years of the 19th century, when patronage was on the decline because power was slipping from the hands of the Rajput princes and new forces were emerging. Sikh power began quickly to dominate the scene but this notwithstanding, the interest taken by the Pahari painters in the Sikhs as patrons and as subjects of painting was slow and cautious, for only very gradually did "Rajput aloofness" yield to "Sikh warmth and affability". In his view, then: "The years 181o to 183o saw the first approach by hill artists to Sikh patrons and the first expression of interest in painting by Sikhs themselves." He draws attention to developments at Guler between 1815 and 182o, and sees in Desa Singh Majithia, the tactful and generous Sikh Governor of the hills, as possibly the earliest patron of painting. However, things went obviously slowly, for Mr. Archer says: "Until the second quarter of the nineteenth century, no painting that is truly Sikh can be said to exist."[31]

We now know a little more about Sikh interest in painting. In fact, with the help of the Pahari diagram that we have spoken of before, this interest can securely be dated back into the 18th century, for Jai Singh and Gurbakhsh Singh Kanhaiya and Jassa Singh Ramgarhia, the three Sikh Chiefs mentioned in it by name, all belonged to that period. The fact that these Chiefs' are the only personal names in the diagram, while all other entries refer to names of states, is no surprise: it is to be explained by the circumstance that these Misaldar chiefs did not belong to any dynasty of rulers with fixed domains and given capital towns. Besides the evidence of the diagram, we now also have visual evidence in support of the interest taken in painting by some of these Chiefs, or at least of the interest taken in them by the Pahari painters. There is that telling painting in the Chandigarh Museum in which Sardar Jai Singh Kanhaiya is seen in the company of several Pahari rulers, including Raj Singh of Chamba, Prakash Chand of Guler, Sansar Chand of Kangra, and other princes and their wazirs.[32] The same subject is treated of in another painting known to us,[33] and there is no mistaking the purport of these paintings, nor who the most important figure in these is. These paintings are clearly devoted to Jai Singh who appears here in a commanding position, even if it is assumed that the painters came from the atelier of Sansar Chand, who was then only a young prince. There are other portraits of Jai Singh, one of them showing him with his young son, Gurbakhsh Singh. Gurbakhsh Singh himself is portrayed at least twice more, once on horseback as a youth of daring, and once as a more grown up figure, holding a bow and arrow in his hands.[34] Jassa Singh Ramgarhia, again, is seen in a portrait in the British Museum,[35] and the Boston Museum has that impressive if badly damaged picture from the 18th century which Dr. Coomaraswamy published many years ago as an "An Assembly of the Sikhs".[36] All this leaves little doubt that the interest of the painters of the hills had already fixed itself in some measure, in the last quarter of the 18th century, on these enterprising, if rough, soldiers of fortune. And none of this comes as a surprise, for the history of the hill states was at this time becoming intertwined with the history of these and other Sikh Chiefs who had established themselves first in the foothills of the Punjab and were now fast assuming a position of ascendancy in the region, alike through conquest and intrigue and division.[37] The power of the Sikh Chiefs, Jai Singh and Jassa Singh, is felt distinctly as we trace the career of Sansar Chand who in his early years had to come to terms with both of them and became involved in the web of power they were weaving in their own interest. The Sikh presence in the hills was considerable, then, and everyone, including the painters, saw this.

For all our awareness of patrons such as these, however, we have had until now, no secure evidence of their painters. Even when we come to the 19th century, to which Dr. Archer devotes such detailed attention, the names of Pahari painters working for Sikh patrons are difficult to come by. The Sikh painters we do hear about: Kishan Singh, Bishan Singh, Kehar Singh, Kapur Singh,[38] even if we know little about them. There are two other names, those of Muslims, which are mentioned: Muhammad Bakhsh and Hasam-ud-din; and the Delhi painter, Azam, also puts in an appearance. But of the Pahari painters whose work for Sikh patrons we mostly see in Sikh subject paintings, we have really very scanty knowledge.

Our information on Pahari painters working in the plains is, however, slowly building up and much of this comes from diverse and interesting sources. Thus, we know now of Devi Ditta, son of Gur Sahai, grandson of Ranjha, of the Seu-Nainsukh family, having migrated from Basohli to Lahore, possibly in the wake of dwindling patronage at the Basohli court. A sequence of entries by him in the registers of the priests at different centres of pilgrimage in North India clearly establishes that he lived at Lahore for some time in the house of Bulaki Missar, in the 'gali' or street of Kanhaiya Kapoor, in the quarter of the town called Machhihatta.[39] In the middle of the century,

Devi Ditta shifted from Lahore to Patiala, apparently because a royal prince there was still in a position to patronise the arts while Lahore had ceased to be effective. In the British Museum, there is still more interesting evidence on Devi Ditta in an inscribed portrait of the great Dogra, Raja Dhian Singh.[40] This shows the Raja receiving something from one "Devi Ditta", presumably none else then the painter of our acquaintance. In the background of this scene stands the Kamlagarh fort (in the Mandi territory) which gives us additional interesting information that the painters often moved with their patrons. Clearly, the Kamlagarh of this picture was not the place where Dhian Singh was resident: but we do know that he was in these environs when Maharaja Sher Singh was in the Mandi hills. Raja Dhian Singh had followed him there in an attempt to press upon him the urgency of some matters of state; in this trip his painter might have gone with him too. In any event, this painting opens up the possibility of our seeing a link between the family of the Dogra and Devi Ditta, the painter.

Another family of artists that we see as serving at Lahore is the family of Purkhu. We know of Purkhu as one of the prominent Pahari artists from the evidence of Baden-Powell who mentions him as a Kangra artist in his account of the manufactures of the Punjab,[41] and this Purkhu we connect with the artist family of Samloti.[42] The genealogical table of the family gives the names of Purkhu's two brothers as Buddhu and Rattu.[43] In an extremely interesting and useful letter-like note that I found inscribed at the back of a drawing of a courtier in the family of the artist Gulabu Ram, a descendant of Purkhu, the artist Buddhu is respectfully addressed by his two brothers, Purkhu and Rattu, who request him for something for themselves "when he goes to Lahore <u>next</u>."[44] Small as this piece of evidence is, it does somehow succeed in connecting this family of Samloti artists with Lahore again, and this connection could, with ease, be traced to the first quarter of the 19th century, a time in which Purkhu himself was evidently active. On Purkhu himself we have the evidence of Fakir Waheeduddin, a descendant of the famous Fakir family which served Maharaja Ranjit Singh. Fakir Waheeduddin speaks of Purkhu of Kangra along with Kehar Singh and Muhammad Baksh among the artists at the Lahore court, presumably with reference to the collection of paintings of the Fakir family some of which he reproduces.[45]

Another Pahari name we know of in the context of Sikh painting is that of the artist Chhajju, apparently the son of Nikka, of whom we hear more a little later in these document. His name occurs in a long verse which goes with a portrait showing one Wasawa Singh with his companions and attandants in a garden party. This portrait is now in a Dutch collection and was published by Dr. Goetz without, however, his identifying the Sikh Sardar in it precisely.[46]

To add to all these names and scraps of information, now comes this group of documents which gives decided substance to our picture of the patronage of the arts at the Sikh court, not only by the Maharaja and the members of the royal family, but also, as was shrewdly suggested by Dr. Archer, by the nobles at the court. If it did not all begin with the Sardars such as Desa Singh, it did at least extend to them. The body of evidence cited here and referred to above is, hopefully, not all that must have existed at one time. Our picture still remains fragmentary, for other painters must also have worked for the Lahore Darbar and its nobles. It is just an accident that we have discovered information in the form of these documents and paintings about this group of painters working for the Sikhs. There must have been many more Pahari painters who came down to the plains and settled there, at least temporarily. In this sense the work of the Punjab Plains is to be seen in a much more definite sense as an extension of the work that was being done in the hills upto the first quarter of the 19th century.

Any account of painting in the Punjab has to be preceded by a background of the history of the Sikh kingdom of Lahore, but this is a story that has been well told before.[47] We know all about the victories and the consolidation and the knitting together of the fabric of an empire, the glory and the excitement of expansion and construction, but also of the pettiness of the intrigue and the treachery that followed it. The characters are well known to us: the great Maharaja himself, Ranjit Singh; his half witted and weak son, Kharak Singh; his youthful grandson, Naunihal Singh, who ruled for but a day. Sher Singh makes a resolute and colourful appearance as a Maharaja, only to be dogged by misfortune, and condemmed to preside over the murderous jealousies that rent the Darbar after the death of the great Maharaja in 1839. The able and dashing Dogras, Gulab Singh, Dhian Singh and Suchet Singh, along with Hira Singh, Ranjit Singh's boy-favorite, we see as controlling affairs both in the plains and in the Jammu Hills for many years, almost to the exclusion of other nobles and arousing the wrath of the ambitous Sandhanwalias. The events are confused and sanguine in turn and have something of the elements of a Greek tragedy. The pattern of intrigue is almost impossible to follow and the thread that is so hard to disentangle is ever so often abruptly cut by a sword. The Sandhanwalias emerge as dominant figures at least in one act of the drama under Sher Singh who himself is shot dead by one of them, his young son is cut into two, and Dhian Singh is murdered. Fate catches up with the Sandhanwalias themselves soon afterwards, for they are cut down one after the other by an irate army played upon by a revengeful Hira Singh, as events move towards the tragic climax, first of one war with the British, then another, and then the annexation of the Punjab to the British Empire in 1849.

These are events of a chilling character and from this blood-soaked chapter of the history of the Punjab after the death of the great Maharaja, few characters emerge with any sympathy. Even during the great Maharaja's lifetime, the pace of events can be seen as fast, for so much happens within a short span of time. In this crowded period, then, very little attention was apt to go, one thinks, to matters such as the patronage of the arts. And yet, quite clearly, nearly everyone had the time for this. The low esteem in which the Maharaja is generally believed to have held the art of painting is wellknown, but this certainly did not keep him from extending patronage in his own way to painters: the first of our documents here is a grant issued with the Maharaja's personal seal. The large number of portraits of him that have survived could again not all have been frowned upon by him, and he did possibly sit for some of the painters to take his likeness.[48] Paintings also made good gifts for the 'Sahibs' with whom the Maharaja had a great deal to do, even if the Sahibs treated such pictures more as curious than as serious works of art.[49] Sher Singh emerges as a fair enthusiast from the account of Dr. Archer and the present documents tend to support this view of him. In one of them, he clearly attaches the painter Gokal to himself through a grant. What comes as entirely new information from these documents is the patronage extended to these painters by the Sandhanwalias. This patronage, in terms of opportunity, is not difficult to understand, however. The Sandhanwalias were men of considerable means and were fairly high in the Maharaja's favour, being descended with him from a common ancestor and, thus, counted as among his closest relatives.[5o] All of them, starting from Amir Singh Sandhanwalia, uncle of Maharaja Ranjit Singh and father of Attar Singh, Jaimal Singh, Budh Singh, Wasawa Singh and Lehna Singh, had their ups and downs in their relationship with the Maharaja, but at times they served him well; some of them fought for him in difficult campaigns and laid their lives down for the kingdom. Jaimal Singh died in the campaign of the Indus in 181o and Budh Singh, whom Lepel Griffin praises as "one of the bravest and most skilful of the Sikh Generals", fought in the Yusufzai country with great distinction. He did give the Maharaja occasion for displeasure, but generally was "a great favourite at the Court". When Wasawa Singh died in 1836, the Maharaja was sad, says the chronicler, Sohan Lal, and remarked:[51] "The Sardar was a forbearing, tolerant, brave and a very useful man. Sardar Attar Singh is a brave and daring person no doubt, but he has a hastiness about him". The 'hasty' Attar Singh who became head of the family after his father's death in 1827, had all the same a string of titles from the Maharaja which read "Ujjal didar, nirmal budh, sardar-i-bawaqar, Kaiser-ul-iqtadar, sarwar-i-giroh-i-namdar, Ali tabai, Shuja-ud-daulah, Sardar Attar Singh, Shamsher-i-Jang Bahadur." In terms of titles, his brother

Lehna Singh did not do badly either,[52] all of which gives us some indication of their standing at the Court. The Sandhanwalias were clearly men of courage and valour, including Ajit Singh, son of Wasawa Singh, but they were apparently not overly-wise and the description "headstrong and rash" which we find applied to them fits them rather neatly. In the mind of the chronicler or the historian of the period, the Sandhanwalia name evokes unpleasant images of a blood-bath which they clearly embarked upon under Sher Singh. To connect this family in our minds with the arts, then, is not easy, and yet nearly all of them find mention in these documents, leaving very little doubt that they took keen interest in painting. The first grant in this series of documents is made by the Maharaja at the recommendation of Sardar Budh Singh. Attar Singh and Lehna Singh equally figure here. Even far away from Lahore, when Ajit Singh is in the Mandi hills, he has time to attend to a matter apparently brought to his notice by the painter, Gokal. All of this changes no part of the violent role that the Sandhanwalias played in the events in the Punjab, and yet they emerge from these documents perhaps as slightly different persons than one saw them as before.

There is no clear information in these papers about the interest taken in painting by the Majithias, Desa Singh and his son, Lehna Singh, even though they possibly had perhaps the best opportunity, after the members of the royal family, to attach to themselves painters from the hills, being the Governors of these regions.[53] The evidence on the subject is of course by no means conclusive, for painters other than these belonging to the family of Nikka could have served them. Here, however, only one document is directly connected with Sardar Lehna Singh Majithia in which he orders a subordinate of his to confer a cash <u>jagir</u> on the painter Harkhu, son of Nikka, in supersession of Fauju. Even here, however, he is acting on behalf of the Lahore authority and not on his own. The indirect involvement of Lehna Singh, Governor of the hills after the death of his father, Desa Singh, in 1832 must of course always have been there with each of these grants, for papers must of necessity have passed through his hands on their way to the junior functionaries. In this way, he must have stood at the centre of much that was going on between the patrons at the Court and these Pahari painters.

IV The Contacts

It is not difficult to speculate on and reconstruct the situation of the painter-family of our documents and the manner in which its members came into contact with the power in the Punjab Plains. We know Nikka to have been settled on a piece of land within his territories in the Rihlu <u>taaluqa</u> by Raja Raj Singh of Chamba. Nikka's holding was not much more than 3o <u>kanals</u> of land but his family, at the time that he settled there coming from Guler, was perhaps sufficiently small to be able to live off the produce of that fertile piece. The patronage extended to Nikka by Chamba could not however have continued entirely undisturbed for long, because Raj Singh's power was shaken by that of the more powerful Sansar Chand of Kangra. The war between Kangra and Chamba in 1794 ended in the death of Raj Singh but Sansar Chand did not succeed in annexing the whole tract of Rihlu, gaining only a few border villages. We do not know if Gaggal, the little village where Nikka's *jagir* was located, became part now of Kangra territory, but it is unlikely that it did, for Gaggal was not a border village and we find later that the contact between the family of Nikka and the royal house of Chamba survived into the 19th century. An interesting note at the back of a painting showing the nether regions of the world, now in the Bhuri Singh Museum at Chamba, gives us fairly clear indication of this.[54] For, this inscription which has been published and is the subject of some difference of opinion among scholars, lists a number of members of this artist-family, including Attra, grandson of Nikka, and others, having been attached "since olden times" to "the royal house of Chamba". In other matters, however, things began to change radically from the very beginning of the 19th century. The year 18o5 saw the invasion of the territories of Kangra by the Gurkhas. This chapter of the history of the hills is well known, for it became a prelude to the later occupation of most of the hills by the Sikh Maharaja of Lahore.[55] The Gurkhas made a dent in the power of Sansar Chand but were not yet able to subdue him. In 18o9, they returned in larger numbers and with the abetment of other hill chiefs who were straining under the yoke of Sansar Chand's growing power and ambition. This time they pressed the Kangra ruler to the wall. He had to appeal to the Maharaja of Lahore to come to his assistance. This assistance he did receive but at a price that was all but too high. For, while the Maharaja helped Sansar Chand to push the Gurkhas back, he revealed his own designs upon this region by demanding the handing over of the prestigious fort of Kangra to him together with the small group, initially, of the sixty-six villages around the fort which used to maintain the garrison of the fort. This, however, was only the thin end of the wedge. Ranjit Singh was there to stay in the hills and gradually, but quite systematically, he began to bend the power of the proud houses of the Rajputs of the hills. The story of his conquest of the hills by power, intrigue and stratagem is known. For our purposes here, it is enough to notice that from the second decade of the century onwards, the overlord of the hills was Ranjit Singh, and the growing slices of his kingdom in the hills were placed under the administration of his trusted *Nazim* of the hills, Desa Singh Majithia.

The change of government in the hills did not, however, mean a complete break with the past, even if it did mean some disruption in the tenor of the life there. This is a point that emerges with fair sharpnes from the accounts in the Settlement Reports and the Gazetteer of the Kangra District.[56] By and large, grants of land which were enjoyed by people under the Rajput chiefs were maintained. There might have been some more demands, a little more injustice at places, and some supplanting of the jagirs[57] of some people in the hills who had fallen out of favour. But Desa Singh Majithia earned a reputation as a mild and just administrator, even if he mostly lived in the plains, away from the hills, and conducted business through his trusted functionaries. It is reasonable to assume that many of the jagirs which had been given by the Rajput chiefs to their nobles and soldiers were maintained on the condition that they transferred their services and allegiance to the new Sikh overlords. These jagirs were obviously difficult for a new power to maintain unless the service now passed on to the new owners of power. The patta of land that Raj Singh of Chamba had, in the first instance, given to Nikka, as we have seen, is no longer traceable, but it is easy to visualise that the grant mentioned that the land was being given as a retainer, as was the practice, for the services of the painter and the members of his family. The words "naukri jagir"[58] might not have been mentioned (muafi[59] or'rent-free tenure'is more likely to have been used), but the import of the grant must have been clear: Nikka was serving, and in consideration of his services, he was settled on this piece of land. When the Sikhs took over - and they clearly took over the group of villages in which Nikka's lands and homestead were located - it must have followed that Nikka was to transfer his services to the new rulers if he wished to keep his lands. We do not know whether he went to Lahore soon after he realised that he could hold on to his jagir only if he made his services available to those who were in a position to maintain or resume it. But he must have gone to Lahore, like so many others, in search of security of tenure, and of new patrons.

At Lahore, or possibly even during a dignitary's visit to the hills, Nikka seems to have caught the eye of Sardar Budh Singh Sandhanwalia who was, through relationship and position, close to the Maharaja himself.[60] An indication of this is available from the very first document in our collection, for while Maharaja Ranjit Singh refers in it to grant 'as of old' to Nikka, he brings in a clear reference to the "recommendation" that was made by Sardar Budh Singh on Nikka's behalf. The situation here is of great interest in many ways. The Sandhanwalia Sardars were men of very considerable means. They enjoyed extensive jagirs of their own through the favour of Ranjit Singh in different parts of the Punjab which they later concentrated, through consolidation, mostly in the district of Amritsar.[61] Had Sardar Budh Singh, or any of his brothers, wanted to do so, Nikka or any other painter could easily have been given a piece of land to settle upon in their own estate. But apparently Nikka was reluctant to shift out of the hills. The folk-songs that tell of the attachment of the inhabitant of the hills to his lovely region with its flowing streams and its limpid vision of the snowy Dhaula Dhar range in the background[62], help to explain the extreme aversion of the hillmen to move out forever. Nikka must have wanted to leave his family undisturbed, and while he made his talent available, he probably insisted on being allowed to continue to enjoy the peace and the quiet of his little homestead in the hills. In any event, even if Nikka was himself required to come away for long periods, he wished that his family be permitted to stay on there. If this was so, then Budh Singh could not have helped Nikka except by asking his relation and master, Ranjit Singh, to accomodate Nikka to the extent asked for by him, even if he was not directly entering the service of the Maharaja himself. It is probable that the value of the jagir that Nikka enjoyed, small as it was, was eventually deducted from the total jagirs enjoyed by the Sandhanwalias: a reference to this will be seen in another document later. It is interesting to notice then that Budh Singh, for all his own wealth, had to depend upon Ranjit Singh for this favour to Nikka, for while he could have paid Nikka any amount that he wanted to in cash, the piece of land that Nikka wanted to hold on to was directly under the Maharaja. It is also not in conceivable that Nikka served both the Sandhanwalias and Ranjit Singh while he was engaged.

All this seems to have happened before A.D. 1825, the year of our first document. This document makes a significant reference to "earlier grants", some of them presumably given by the Rajput chiefs, and others by Ranjit Singh himself.[63] This document is thus only a confirmatory grant: it is not clearly the original patta given for the first time to Nikka by a Sikh authority. Had it been so, the details of the piece of land enjoyed in perpetuity by Nikka's family would have been mentioned as in a zimn of a Mughal farman.[64] Here the details of the grant are taken for granted and only the value of the jagir, Rs. 125 per annum, is mentioned as indication of its quantum. The document bearing the personal seal of the Maharaja is followed by another (No. II), this time issued by Raja Dhian Singh who must have found it necessary to address the Kardar[65] of Rihlu, Ganda Mal, by name. The fact that the Kardar is addressed directly both by the Maharaja and his chief minister is not without interest. One would have normally thought that an order like this would be routed through the Nazim of the hills, Desa Singh Majithia. Apparently, however, the power at Lahore not only retained but exercised the right to directly intervene in these matters and conferred or issued grants of this order directly. The two documents relating to Nikka must both be seen not as pattas or original grants, but simply as parwanas or official letters which Nikka equipped himself with to show the interest of the granting authority in him.

It is quite possible that these were required to be produced in 1846, when the British took this region over, for them to go into the question of whether grants like these were to be maintained or resumed. If the pattas were indeed presented in this fashion, they were apparently not returned, or were later lost, for they are no longer in the family collection.

Nikka does not find mention in the next document (No.III), a copy of a 'patta' of Maharaja Ranjit Singh which is dateable to A.D. 1836. His death must have occured between 1825, the year of the issue of the first two documents, and 1836. This is confirmed by other evidence: the records of the priests at pilgrim centres show that Nikka's remains were taken to Haridwar for immersion in A.D. 1833.[66] At this time, the three sons of Nikka, Harkhu, Gokal and Chhajju were active. We find Gokal receiving the attention of Sardar Ajit Singh Sandhanwalia[67] in 1836 (No. V). To the grant of land worth Rs. 125 per annum which was enjoyed by Nikka, we now find an addition of Rs. 1oo per annum. This new grant by the Maharaja seems to have been given in the taaluqa[68] of Haripur-Guler,[69] whereas the earlier grant was in the taaluqa of Rihlu.[7o] The value of the grant thus goes up to Rs. 225 and it is spread over lands which fall in two separate though neighbouring taaluqas. This grant by the Maharaja mentions an interesting fact to which allusion has been made before. It states that the signatures of Sardar Lehna Singh Sandhanwalia should be obtained in connection with the parwana issued to Gokal and "the amount should be adjusted" (in the accounts of the said Sardars). Fairly clearly, the situation that had obtained under Nikka continues. Nikka's sons persist in their desire to retain their jagir in the hills, even though they are serving their patrons, the Sandhanwalias, in the plains of the Punjab. The possibility of their receiving a grant within the plains estates of the Sandhanwalias must again have been there, but is not used. Since the painters' lands are situated in the Maharaja's khalisa territories,[71] therefore, the Maharaja orders that the deduction of these amounts be duly made from the accounts of the jagirs of the Sandhanwalias.

In 1837, we find Gokal mentioned as "a servant"[72] of Sardar Attar Singh who was the head of the Sandhanwalia family now, after the death of his father, Sardar Amir Singh, in 1827. It is reasonable to assume that Gokal, along with his brothers, was serving the whole family of the Sandhanwalias, for just a little later, we find a clear statement that others besides Gokal were employed by them. The unsigned letter addressed to Sardar Lehna Singh (Majithia) explicitly states that Harkhu is in the employment of the Sardars; the letter pleads the case of Chhajju; and we are on sure ground that all the three brothers were in the service of the Sandhandwalias. In 184o, we find Ajit Singh Sandhanwalia continuing to take interest in the jagirs of the painters. A document (No. VI) which does not mention the amount of the new grant, indicates that additional land had been given to Gokal in the taaluqa of Ramgarh[73] which was, once again, not far from the other family holdings, being just across the khud from Rajol. The painters now were apparently consolidating their gains: their holdings were now in the three taaluqas of Rihlu, Haripur and Ramgarh.

These were the years when serious trouble began to brew between Maharaja Sher Singh and the Sandhanwalias. The Maharaja had never been looked upon with much favour by these powerful vassals, and a clear split of interests took place. The great Maharaja had died in 1839 to be followed by his son and grandson soon. An elaborate and expensive game was being played out between Sher Singh, the Sandhanwalias, and the Dogra brothers. In the patronage of painting, however, Sher Singh decided to take the initiative into his own hands, as it were. In 1841 he takes charge of Gokal. In a document issued by him, he states firmly that the painter who was "formerly in the service of the Sandhanwalia Sardars" had now entered his service. The follow-up action after this document is impressive. The amount of the grants to the painters is left undisturbed, but Bawa Lachhman Singh,[74] apparently a subordinate of Sardar Lehna Singh Majithia, Nazim of the hills after the death of his father, issued letters to the Kardars of the different taaluqas in question, not to disturb the painters in the enjoyment of their jagirs. The tone of the letters is clear and firm and the swiftness of this action reflects the interest perhaps of the new patron in seeing to it that his "servants" are not unduly harassed.

In 1842, we find interest being taken in the painter Harkhu by Sardar Lehna Singh Majithia himself. In a document (No.XI) he orders that the naqad jagir or cash annual grant which was formerly in conferment upon the painter Fauju (who might have died in this year) was to be transferred to Harkhu in the future. Perhaps Harkhu had managed now to attach himself somehow to the powerful and wise Governor.[75]

There is some indication that things were not going well between the painter-brothers themselves. One of the documents (No.XII) shows that Chhajju had appropriated the whole piece of land in one taaluqa.This was resented by Gokal who made an appeal against this and orders are issued that Chhajju was to share the land with Gokal in equal measure. The document is uncompromising in its intent: it says that this division of land should not be merely nominal. Land good in quality should be equally divided as much as the land which was poor in quality. In fact, the document goes further and says that the produce from the land, possibly the crop just harvested, should also be divided equally between Chhajju and Gokal. It is interesting to see that the land granted is referred to here as an "ʾaimma", a term used generally though not exclusively for religious grants in the Mughal times.[76]

Chhajju seems to have struck an uneasy patch of time at this point. The case of murder instituted against him earlier, the admonition to him that he is to share his lands with his brother, are fair indications. We also have a note written by Narayan Chaudhari (No.XIII) to a functionary, possibly in Lahore, recommending the case of Chhajju. In this, Narayan Chaudhari who was approached by Chhajju in his difficulty says that the 'salary' which is due to Chhajju may be released to him.

In 1843 we find Gokal firmly mentioned again as being in the service of the court of Lahore. The tiny little document that mentions this specifically contains the order that his name should be entered by the mutasaddis[77] in the records of the Daftar-i-Mualla[78] on terms which are clearly spelled out. It is just conceivable that Chhajju, like Gokal, was also similarly in the employment of the Lahore Darbar, then presided over by Sher Singh, on similar terms mentioning, besides the grant of land, the cash salary to be drawn and the rations to be issued.

Between 1843 and 1845, from which we have the next document, events moved rapidly and, as we have seen, along a sanguine path. Sher Singh was shot dead by Lehna Singh Sandhanwalia and his son Pratap Singh cut down by Ajit Singh. Raja Dhian Singh also died at their hands to be followed soon after by the Sandhanwalias themselves. Things had taken such a grave and anarchical turn for all that men's minds longed for the relative peace and quiet of the days of the great Maharaja. There were many who began to feel out of tune with the new and turbulent spirit of these times: among these was Sardar Lehna Singh Majithia who deemed it wise at this juncture to leave the Punjab, ostensibly on a long pilgrimage to Haridwar and Benares etc. Speculation was rife as to the reasons that made him leave at this point of time in 1844, and his move was less than appreciated by many at the Lahore Court who did not regard him with a kind eye.[79] But Lehna Singh had made his mind up, and perhaps wisely. With his going, the hills lost, as did the Lahore Court, a prudent and sagacious man. He was to reappear later in the Punjab, but not to come back to his charge in the hills. In his absence, it was his half-brother, Ranjodh Singh, who received the charge of the hills for a short time.[80] Ranjodh Singh is not the most endearing character in the annals of Sikh history, but at this juncture, for good or ill, he was clearly in a position of power in the hills even if it was only for a little more than a year. The two documents which bear the seal of Ranjodh Singh in the present collection (No. XV) confirm the grant to Gokal in the taaluqa of Haripur etc. This was only to be expected. A change in Governorship in the hills did not necessarily imply a change in the status of all the grantees and jagirdars in that region.

The next years saw drastic developments. The first Anglo-Sikh war came in 1846. With the history of that war this narrative is not naturally concerned, but the end of the war saw a profound change in the fortunes of the hills. By the terms of the treaty that ended it, the Sikh authority in the hills was replaced by that of the British for, among other things, the Mahraja ceded to "the Honourable Company in perpetual sovereignty, all his forts, territories, and rights, in the Doab, or country, hill and plain, situate between the rivers Beas and Sutlej". Sikh rule had lasted in the hills for less than four decades and was now over. The direct take-over of the hill regions by the British extended only to such areas as were formerly part of the Sikh domains, leaving other states such as Mandi, Kulu and Chamba to continue to remain under their own Rajput princes, but the lands enjoyed by the painters who we treat of here passed clearly into British hands. From the moment of their assuming authority in these parts, the British set resolutely to work. The swiftness with wich they succeeded in establishing a clear order in the hills is impressive. Among the many questions that faced them was the question of what to do with the _jagirs_ in the hills. Quite decisively the matter was probed into, examined, discussed and then decided upon.[81] There was discussion, but no faltering of any kind. The general principle that things from the earlier reign should be changed as little as possible, at least initially, was kept but modifications were also made. The British officers gave serious thought apparently to many aspects of the matter and the length at which the 'jagir cases of the Kangra Hills', as they were generally called, were discussed is indicative of their desire to evaluate their position carefully, especially vis-a-vis the important _jagirdars_ of the area whose loyalty or otherwise might have made a vital difference to the stability of the new regime. But the justification of continuing minor or service _jagirs_ was called by them into question. The recommendations sent by the Resident to the Governor General for his consideration in respect of all _jagir_ cases in the hills make highly instructive reading.[82] The _jagirs_ were clearly classified into seven different categories, based upon principles that rendered "the adjustment of all claims easy and intelligible". There were those which were not to be touched at all: these were to remain with their holders in perpetuity. There were others which were to be treated only for life and were to be allowed to pass on to the successor of the incumbent upon the payment of concessional land-rent. There were other _jagirs_ which were to be resumed summarily. A large number of petty _jagirs_, not specifically meant for religious establishments, fell into a separate category. The religious grants were not disturbed: the British correctly estimated the sentiment of people on the subject. The so-called 'service-_jagirs_' were all individually examined and decided upon. We do not have any separate statement in the categories of _jagirs_ about those which were enjoyed by the painters and the like, but then these _jagirs_ must have been to small and insignificant for them to find any prominent mention in the discussions. It appears, however, that while their jagirs were not summarily resumed, the decision taken followed generally that which applied to service-jagirs: the incumbent holders were to be allowed to continue to hold for their lives, in some cases free of rent, in others subject to the payment of "quarter jumma" - payment of concessional land-rent which was one fourth of what it would have been for others. Upon the death of the holder, the lands in most of these cases were to be resumed, assessed at full value, and the descendant given the opportunity to engage at these terms. In other words, while the right to the lands was not to be denied to the family, a right it had enjoyed for serveral generations, the State revenue was not to be permitted to suffer on this account.

The four documents from the British period which might initially appear repetitive and inconsequential, belong to the years 1846 and 1847. But they are all included here for each of them has something somewhat different to say than the previous one. In 1846, matters regarding jagirs were being worked out, but tentative decisions had been taken regarding the jagirs of these painters. On the 8th of July, 1846, the painter Damodar deposits Rs. 13 in the State treasury: the taking over of the hills by the British seems roughly to have coincided, in the family of Nikka, with the death of Damodar's father, Gokal. Damodar being the elder of the two sons of Gokal, was allowed to engage for the land in the possession of his branch of the family.[83] The amount that he deposits on the 8th of July appears however only to be a roughly calculated sum which was to be revised later. This money was in a sense to be kept in trust for him in deposit. Only two months later, on the 1oth of September, the quantum of the land-rent due from Damodar for the rabi' crop of Samvat 19o3 seems to have been decided upon, and he receives a receipt for the amount of Rs. 15, annas 6 and 6 pies. The revenue due on the kharif crop, which always tends in the hills to be more than that on the rabi' crop, is deposited by him again on the 1st of November to the extent of Rs. 42 and 2 annas. The amount for the kharif crop had been clearly split into two instalments, one to be paid in November and the other to be paid in January of the following year. This is a practice which, interestingly enough, continues in the hills to the present day. The painter Chandu Lal and his family pay the revenue due on the kharif crop in two instalments, much as his ancestor did 125 years before him. The last of the British documents is dated the 27th of January, 1847. In this Damodar pays the second instalment due on the kharif crop: an amount of Rs. 43, 1 anna and 6 pies. In all, then, for the kharif crop of Samvat 19o3, the amount paid by Damodar comes to Rs. 85, 3 annas and 6 pies. These receipt are issued individually in the name of Damodar, since he was paying this amount not for the holdings of the entire family including the branch of Chhajju and his sons, Attra and Saudagar, but only for the lands which were with him and his brother Ramdayal.

The documents which serve as receipts for land-revenue paid by Damodar contain brief, austere statements. There are understandably no literary flourishes about them; the Persian is gone and comes in only in a vestigial form in some of the phrases; the sar-i-nama[84] on the top of the documents has again disappeared. All that remains is a factual statement, clear and impersonal: the lands are with the family still but are no longer held rent-free. This is a fact which could not have been much to the liking of Damodar and his family. But, perhaps, the gain for the family was not too poor either, for the British regime had conferred on these owners of lands, rights of proprietorship which they had not possessed in theory for generations, and had given to them, in addition, a security of tenure which they had not had under either the Sikhs or the Rajput Chiefs.

The tragic element in the situation, however, is not the amount of land revenue that Damodar and his family had to pay, but the fact that the painters were now completely on their own, as it were. They were like any other small landholders. The patronage which they had received from the ruling houses of the hills and the plains of the Punjab had been completely withdrawn. The 'Sahibs' had obviously no use for Damodar and the like. From them came no encouragement of any kind. Their esteem for the painters' work was generally low and their interest severely limited. All that the painters could usefully do, as far as the British interest in painting was concerned, was to turn out heaps of sets, swiftly drawn and rather coldly rendered, of castes and trades and professions that go by the name of 'Company Painting'.[85]

In this rather heartless situation, the 19th century painter had to fend for himself. Wherever he could, he still turned towards princely patronage. With Lahore becoming inhospitable, we see Devi Ditta shifting from there. In 1866, we find him in Patiala, serving Raja Mohinder Singh.[86] There were still some possibilities at Patiala, for its rulers were men of means and laid claims to taste. To Patiala, then, repaired painters of other families and areas: the artist Biba of Guler also shifted to Patiala;[87] so did a family of Muslim painters, among them Basharatullah.[88] A family of painters from Alwar is also known to have moved to Patiala becoming responsible for the coming together of the Rajasthani and Pahari kalams that we find in the frescos of the Shish Mahal at Patiala.[89] The artist Saudagar, cousin of Damodar, was probably itinerant for a while. One entry of Haridwar records a visit of his to Haridwar from Garhwal where he might have worked for some time.[90] Attra worked for a patron nearer home, the Raja of Chamba, as evidenced by the inscription at the back of the painting in the Bhuri Singh Museum earlier referred to. Presumably, the Chamba house also afforded patronage to Saudagar who is the author of the last of the documents in the present collection, a petition to a Maharani. It is by no means certain who the addressee of this rather plaintive but fairly-skilled draft missive is. But it is not unlikely that the Maharani in question was the Regent Mother who presided over the affairs of Chamba at the death of Raja Charat Singh, when her son was still in his infancy. In any event, the peregrinations of Devi Ditta and Biba and Attra and Saudagar are clearly symptomatic of the fact that in its last phase, the art of the hills was still looking around for patronage from the princes. But this was a search that could not go on for long: what was being sought was not there, and those who sought it were predestined to lose.

V The Terms; The Situation

The economic condition of the Indian artist has of recent years been a matter of considerable interest and, in the absence of much definite evidence, some speculation. From the Pahari area, the general impression that one receives about this condition is that which is reflected in a letter written by the artist Shiba to his patron, Maharaja Sansar Chand: skilfully worded as that letter is, diplomatic and suave in its tone, it still forcefully drives the point home about the state of want in which the painter lived.[91] There is a throbbing note of urgency in Shiba's petition, and when he asks the Maharaja to allow him to depart because his resources are exhausted, his dues are embezzled by a dishonest functionary, and no one is willing to advance him loans anymore, one sees in him perhaps a representative figure, forced to survive on little more than dedication to his work.

From these documents the general view that one gets of the economic situation of this family of artists is, however, different. The phrase that one encounters so often here, "land worth Rs. 225 a year" (especially in the later documents) possibly means an area of land the produce from which, free of rent, is worth Rs. 225 a year. This is not a negligible holding.[92] But if the phrase signifies, as the use of the word <u>jagir</u> might suggest, "an area of land the revenue on the produce of which would amount to Rs. 225 per annum", then this holding must indeed appear considerable, although not quite as large as one might initially think considering that, at a rough estimate, in those times anything between one-third to one-half of the value of the produce went to the state in the form of land revenue. By this reckoning, the value of the total produce form the land could have been between Rs. 450 and Rs. 675 per annum. But this again would be the extent of the gross value: much was to be deducted from it further in the form of a host of imposts, some legal and recognized, others oppressive and of the invention of the local set of functionaries. The vexatious nature of these dues, and the variety of them are a recurring theme in the literature on the subject from the early days of British India when the relatively simple and more efficient system introduced by the British was being constantly contrasted with the confusion and the oppressiveness of the system under their predecessors.

Everything considered, however, the painters of these documents do not seem to have done badly for themselves at all. For one thing, their holdings show a constant upward trend. From the poor thirty kanals or so that Nikka held from Raj Singh of Chamba in the 18th century, their fortunes seemd to have steadily gained. Even from the year 1825, when Nikka's grant from Ranjit Singh mentions the amount of Rs. 125, and a holding only in the taaluqa of Rihlu, there is a progressive augmentation of their possessions, first in taaluqa Haripur, then in taaluqa Ramgarh. There is little doubt that their patrons were well pleased with Harkhu and Gokal and Chhajju. The painter Chandu Lal, grandson of Ramdayal (brother of Damodar to whom the British officials issued receipts for land revenue in 1846-47), recalls that as late as the time of his grandfather, the share of their family in the holdings of land was 44 ghumaons of land.[93] This, by usual standards, is a handsome holding and if this is taken as an index to the holdings of the other branches of the family descended from Nikka, the family must indeed have been in fair circumstance.

The modest fortunes that the sons of Nikka made in these grants cannot necessarily be seen as bearing a direct relationship to the quality of their work. The style of the family is not our concern in the present study, but whatever has survived of the work of Harkhu or Gokal or Chhajju does not lead one to the conclusion that their work was superior in any way to that of Nikka, their father, or Nainsukh, their grandfather, both of whom probably lived on considerably less. While the work of these three painters is decidedly competent, a certain hardness has already entered it.[94] There is an ornate tendency in it, a desire to embroider and expand the small core of excellence that is in the work. If the work of the painters, therefore, is not of that high a quality which their less affluent forerunners commanded, the answer to the paradox lies possibly in the greater affluence of the patrons of these latter-day painters. There cannot be any useful comparison between the resources of the Sikh Court of Lahore, or even of its distinguished nobles, and the severely limited resources of the Rajput houses of the hills. The Sikhs could pay much more, and their retained artists were happy to take advanatage of this situation.

The words that are used to describe the holdings of the painters need a word of comment. We hear of them as jagir, muafi and in one case, 'aimma. The jagir of this usage is, however, to be understood in a somewhat different sense than the word generally implies. The normal connotation of a jagir would be the assignment of the revenue due to the state from a piece of land to an individual.[95] A jagirdar, thus, in the Mughal times, would be one who collected and enjoyed, instead of the State, the land revenue due from certain lands because this amount had been assigned to him for a consideration. The association of the word jagir is also generally with large holdings or with control over considerable areas. And one does not normally think of the painters as jagirdars in the manner in which, in British India, the Rajas of Lambagraon or Guler or Nurpur became jagirdars after the cession of the hills to the British by the Sikhs. Yet the word jagir is consistently used, leading one to the conclusion that it bore no relationship to the size of the holding.

The jagirs held by the painters appear to differ significantly from the usual jagirs that we hear of in the Mughal period. In this case, the painters do not seem to have collected the land-revenue from specified lands; they seem to have been in possession of the lands and entitled, in a proprietory sense, to the produce of these lands, free of rent.[96] The reference to the sharing of the 'ghalla-i-aimma' between brothers in one of the documents (No. XII) leaves one in little doubt about this. One also gets indication of this from the insistent reference to the quality of the land being given to the painters: this could have been important only if the painters were to be in its possession and to enjoy its produce.

The word muafi[97] also occurs as a description of the grants in some of these documents, but whenever it does, it is difficult to distinguish between it and a jagir, unless it be that a muafi entitled its owner only to a remission of land revenue and not of other dues. So clear a distinction did not, it appears, however, exist between a muafi and a jagir and possibly both terms were used somewhat loosely. Broadly speaking, the jagirs held by the painters were service-jagirs, a term which is often used in British discussions of the matter, which recognized the right of an artisan or worker to be maintained by the State in return for the services that he rendered to the State or the community. The examples of 'service-jagirs' frequently cited in British correspondence are those that were enjoyed by artisans and craftsmen like weavers, cobblers, oilmen. Theoretically, the painters also belonged to this category, although they are never singled out for mention in the references to service-jagirs. Hopefully, they were considered to be above these workers and 'menials'!

The use of the word aimma, as has been noticed before, is interesting because in the popular usage it must have meant a rent-free grant of any kind, not specifically religious.[98] Even now, the painter Chandu Lal refers with some pride to the 'Āme' that his forefathers enjoyed, without having the slightest clue that the Pahari 'āmā' is only a corrupted derivation from the Persian 'aimma'.

At one place in these documents (No. XI), the expression naqad jagir is employed in the sense of a recurring, cash grant per annum. This is really in the nature of a stipend that Harkhu gets in place of Fauju as per the parwana issued by Sardar Lehna Singh Majithia. The intention in the document is quite clear: the word 'mablagh' alone is here seen as preceding the amount, thus being related to the cash sum alone.

From the point of view of determining the terms on which the painters were formally engaged, the little parwana addressed to the mutasaddis of the 'Daftar-i-Mualla' is possibly the most informative. It mentions that the painter Gokal was to be entitled to three different categories of payment while he was in service. The first was his rasad, the second a cash salary per mensem, and the third the value of the jagir which he enjoyed more or less in perpetuity. The information about the rasad comes in confirmation of the oral evidence from the painters that whenever they were working away from there homes, the patrons issued to them 'enormous' quantities of rasad or rations to maintain them.[99] The rations were enough and to spare, so that the painters often sent quantities of them home. Probably the substance of this oral information is correct, even allowing for the fondness of the painter of today for days gone by. The quantum of the rasad mentioned here is unfortunately not entirely clear. As I have been able to read it, it is given as "six and a half seers". This can only be the rasad that was issued everyday: for a month these rations were too meagre, and the idea of a weekly issue was perhaps not known. For a daily issue, the quantity does seem to be generous and in excess of the needs of an individual. It is not unlikely, however, that the weight mentioned is in kachā seers, a measure with which we were familiar till yesterday and which amounted to a little more than one half of the quantity in 'pucca seers'.

The reading of the cash salary during the period of service in this document is again not free of doubt, but it probably is given as Rs. 3o per mensem. This is again on the generous side as far as payments to craftsmen are concerned, if the petition of Saudagar to the Maharani (No. XX) is any indication. It is interesting in this context to recall that the Gazetteer of the Kangra District mentions the rate of wages to skilled workers in the 2nd half of the 19th century to be half a rupee per diem.[1oo] If the painter Saudagar was being bracketed with other silled workers such as weavers and embroiderers etc., then the quantum of cash pay to him, Rs. 15 per mensem, becomes easier to understand.

The third category of compensation mentioned is perhaps the jagir land. The area of the land or its monetary equivalent is not specified in this document, presumably because it was known and had been determined earlier in other pattas and the like. Here the mention of the jagir land is brought in as a reminder of the fact that the other payments were in addition to the land grants and not in substitution of them. There is naturally no mention of any other kind of compensation such as gifts or rewards to the painter, but in the nature of things, even if these were sometimes considerable, one would not expect them to be included in the formal terms upon which a painter was engaged.

It is fair to assume that when this document is issued in favour of Gokal, it is understood that he comes to Lahore and settles down there to work for the Court. Even earlier than this, he had entered the service of Maharaja Sher Singh, as evidenced by a parwana (No.VIII). But then he might have continued to work mostly at home, like he probably used to for the Sandhanwalia Sardars to whom he was attached earlier. The difference between the wording of the earlier parwana in his favour by Sher Singh, which simply confirms his earlier land grants, and the precise, formal terms upon which he is engaged according to this little note, may be that the expectation now is that he will stay at the Court, away from his family home, for stretches of time. The formal nature of this document of engagement is reflected interestingly, again, in the fact that Gokal is fully identified here, with the names of his father and grandfather, Nikka and Nainsukh, being brought in carefully and the place of his ordinary residence, Rihlu, indicated.[101] This is the only document in the entire collection, as it exists at present, which gives these details. In no other parwana is the parentage of any of the painters identified.

With the last document in this group, we are back again in a situation of want, as it were. Saudagar pleads earnestly to the Maharani for an upward revision in his monthly emoluments. The compensation that his father used to receive, as he says, in the form of "generous rewards" in the time of "the late Maharaja" had now presumably dried up, because the infant ruler could not perhaps exercise judgment to recognise merit in works of art on his own and thus offer rewards. Saudagar had thus to live on the pittance of Rs. 15 per mensem which, he laments, is not enough for the guzara of himself and his family. In some ways we get the feeling that the palmy days of the family are over. There is in this letter an echo somehow of the words of Shiba to Sansar Chand.

(B)

Even during the Sikh period, however, when, at least on paper, the painter was in reasonably good circumstance, his situation was in fact not all that easy. His position as a petty jagirdar is unlikely to have been entirely comfortable, for he must have had at least his share, if not more, of the difficulties that minor jagirdars and muafidars experienced in general at the hands of local functionaries. The tribulations of petty holders of land were many. Even when we examine the situation of considerably more prosperous and influential land-holders in the Mughal and Sikh times, persons such as the Jogi Mahants of Jakhbar and the Vaishnavas of Pindori, there is clear evidence that they met with resistance or interference ever so often in the enjoyment of their grants from local officials: indeed, the point of many of the published documents in their collections is to admonish the local officials not to offer such interference or obstruction.[102] The Mahants were at least men of means and piety in a society in which religion was still a very strong force. Compared to them the painters must been in an infinitely weaker position. To the corrupt and oppressive local functionaries, they must have appeared as persons from whom no gain accrued except to the rulers and nobles, and whose holdings cut into their opportunities to make a dishonest rupee or so. In the Sikh period, the situation of the minor jagirdars was notoriously poor. It was one thing for a person to obtain the grant of a jagir from Lahore, and entirely another for him to convert that grant into a fact and to hold on to his jagir once he managed to come into its actual possession.[103] Right had ever so often to yield to the might of the local functionaries whose private interests suffered everytime that a jagir within their territories was confirmed or enhanced.

It may not be without interest here to try and reconstruct the processes and the channels through which the painter who received a jagir had to pass, in order to understand his total situation better. There was, first, the all-important patta which had to be got issued after a grant was, perhaps orally, conferred. This patta was to be a precise and detailed document which had to be duly entered in the State records, and the obtaining of it must have been no easy matter if the situation prevalent even today is taken as a rough guide. The patta itself had to pass through several offices as the endorsement on the back of some of these would indicate: everywhere signatures had to be affixed, dates entered, entries compared.[104] The painter must then have had to follow the matter up with the Governor, and mild and benevolent as he generally might have been, delays at his end can easily be visualised. The most difficult of his trials must however have been at the level of the Kardar who was the principal officer of the pargana.[105] The Kardars are singled out in the early British records for mention as possibly the most rapacious and the most dishonest of officials. Their duties were extensive, being both military and fiscal, and they were officially entitled to certain levies upon the population within their spheres of activity; they must therefore have had special dislike for anyone who was in favour with their superiors and had thus a backing which interfered with their generally unfettered authority. The Kardar as a corrupt individual is to be seen perhaps as beyond redemption and one can envisage without much effort the problem of the painter in getting past him untouched.

It is the series of difficulties in actually holding on to their jagir lands and enjoying the produce thereof which explains the necessity for the painters to run up every now and then to the Maharaja or a high official to obtain what are in effect letters of admonition addressed to the local officials. The *amils*, the *qanungos*, the *chaudharis*,[106] had all either to be appeased by the painters or to be reminded by them that they were not without support in the higher echelons. A form of pleasant and inexpensive gratification might conceivably have been the painter's offering an occasional painting as a 'gift', or agreeing to do a portrait of the functionary in question. A great many of the uniscribed paintings and sketches of persons of low or no rank exist, and some of them must undoubtedly owe their existence to this situation.[107] But possibly much more effective than this must have been either a gratification in cash or a letter from a superior authority. The letter of recommendation or '*sifarishi khat*' which is such a necessary weapon to wield against bureaucracy in the India of today has obviously a long history. While many of the *parwanas* are ostensibly directives, the *ruqqa* written by Chaudhari Narayan to Lala Sohna Mal (No.XIII), asking him to help Chhajju in the matter of drawing his pay from the *toshakhana* is the kind of document that must so often have been sought by the painters. On occasions, a noble who had no formal title to issue letters such as these in the Kangra territory would also write to the local functionaries, using his general rank and prestige at the Court as a lever. The letters by Ajit Singh Sandhanwalia to the Kardars of Rihlu and so on would thus appear anywhere else to be unwelcome interference in official affairs, but in the situation that obtained, letters such as these were matters of routine. The most interesting of the recommendatory letters is the one addressed to Lehna Singh Majithia on behalf of the painter Chhajju (No.VII) who had got himself into a serious scrape and was accused of murder. The writer of that grandiloquent missive makes bold to say that he has conducted 'personal enquiries' into the affair and finds Chhajju innocent. What is more, he seems to say that because Chhajju, with his brother Harkhu, is in the employment of the writer, he is deserving of every consideration.

One of the problems the painter must have had was that the local officials must have treated his *jagir* on a par with other service-*jagirs* in the area. An irksome part of life for the ordinary cultivor and minor land-holder in the hills was his liability to be pressed into service for *begar*, forced unpaid labour.[108] *Begar* was of different kinds and was imposed as a matter of course. There were many things that needed to be done: loads had to be carried, fodder provided, letters delivered, and so on. For all this the institution of *begar* came in handy for those who were at the benefiting end of the service. The very first *parwana* from Maharaja Ranjit Singh in Nikka's favour clearly specifies that the painter's *jagir* was to be treated as exempt from the imposition of *kar* and *begar*, but the painter could not have had it that easy. Used as the local officials were to demanding this service from just about everyone, the painters must have had to approach the superior power repeatedly to gain letters in their favour certifying and emphasizing that their *jagir* was exempt from this imposition. The practice of *begar* was in any case an indignity, and especially for a painter who was involved with delicate things, it must have appeared as an unbearable burden. We must recall to our minds the story told in the families of Pahari painters that a master painter, when he went out, did not even carry his own water-bowl for fear that the constant bending of the fingers around it would coarsen his hand![109]

Begar apart, we find a reference in one of these documents (No. VI) to the imposition of levies such as *tambul* and *bhati*. The exact nature of these levies is not known, but they were perhaps some kind of customary payments of 'contributions which were extracted from the villagers. On this account, the painter received *khalish-i-beja*, unjust harassment, and this document admonishes the local official to desist from offering it. In one case (No. II), the word *ta'addi* is used in the sense of violence being shown to the painter or his family and this is pointed out as strongly undesirable by the superior, apparently at the instance of the painter.

Since some of the *parwanas* appear, on surface, to be repetitive in character, it is useful to speculate on the circumstances which necessitated the issue of these from time to time.[110] The issue of a *patta* recording a grant for the first time is of course understandable; even though we have none of these in the present collection, they must have been issued to form the basis for later grants and letters etc. This grant needed to be renewed or reconfirmed when the grantor died or ceased to be effective. This is again understandable, because the grants were mostly held from individuals and not, as it were, from the State. This is very much in accordance with the Mughal practice when each Emperor who succeeded to the throne reviewed, in theory, all grants issued by his predecessor and confirmed, modified or resumed them. Another occasion for the re-issue of a grant would be the death of the grantee. His son or successor was not automatically to inherit the grant: the matter was open and even though most often the grant was allowed to continue, the grantor had theoretically the option to discontinue it.

Some of the documents have little to do however with any of the three circumstances indicated above; they are simply reminders to the local functionaries by their superiors that the grants were effective and the painter still in favour. It is not unlikely that the painters themselves, out of a prevailing sense of insecurity, were eager to arm themselves with as many confirmatory letters as possible. These always came in handy. When a patron came to the hills on a tour or on a visit to a sacred place of pilgrimage in the neighbourhood, one can see the painter using the opportunity to present himself and to obtain the favour of receiving a fresh confirmatory or commendatory *parwana*. When Sher Singh is in the Datarpur region, or Ajit Singh Sandhanwalia goes up to Mandi, near the salt mines of Drang, the painter appears there too.

Another occasion for the issue of parwanas was the conferment of an additional grant. Then of course authority was needed by the painter for presenting to the local officials in support of the new grant. A letter or document must, again, have been issued in the event of the restoration of a resumed grant. It is interesting in this connection to notice that the word 'waguzar' finds frequent mention in these documents and may lead to the belief that it is used in the sense of "the restoration of a grant", implying that the grant had been resumed earlier. In the hills, especially during the Sikh period, the resumption of jagirs could not have been a very rare occurrence. However, the impression that one receives from the short intervals at which these confirmatory letters are issued is that the grants were not being 'restored' as such every now and then. On the other hand, the word 'waguzar' was perhaps being used in the sense of 'confirmed'.[111] The mention in a grant then of a land as 'waguzar' would mean that it was in conferment already and not that it was being restored after a period of withdrawal or resumption.

The general situation, as far as these painters were concerned, appears to have been that the patrons kept changing, difficulties were by no means small, but they as a group did manage not only to survive but also to do well for themselves. But this, only as long as there was any degree of interest in their work. With the coming of the British, it is the change in the last circumstance that altered things drastically for them. The affluence of the painter might have remained unaffected under the British; it might even have increased a little keeping in view the new security of their tenures, but interest in their work rapidly diminished, and disappeared altogether after a while. This was the end virtually of painting in these parts. Undoubtedly other factors were also in operation: factors such as the change in techniques, the popularity of the larger format of oil paintings, a change of pace in life itself. But it is difficult to escape the impression that the withdrawal of patronage was at least as important a factor as any other that led to the end of a whole period of painting.

(C)

This group of documents taken together presents evidence that is not as full as one would have wished it to be. There are gaps in the documents and some of the points do not emerge completely clearly. Ideally, one would have wanted to look at the original pattas which formed the basis of the parwanas and the like, which now form the major part of this collection. But presumably these pattas had to be produced before the British authorities by the painters in support of their claims when the British took over. The original pattas may well have been demanded by the new officers who viewed virtually everything with suspicion. In any case, they did want to make sure, for their desire to rely on traditional evidence or hearsay must have been only negligible. They did not have the advantage of having roots in the soil thus understanding instinctively, as it were, the way things had operated before their regime. Documentary proof was what they most demanded.

The British apparently did, however, at the time that they were looking at the original grants presented by various land-holders, issue to them certified copies of the grants whenever demanded. This is indicated, for instance, by the copy of tha _patta_ of Maharaja Ranjit Singh (No. III) which was given on the 11th of June, 1846 to the members of our painter-family. This copy was duly authenticated by the seal of the Agent to the Governor-General. There is an interesting little note on the top right of this copy mentioning the amount of "Rs. 14, 11 annas". While this seemingly does not bear any relationship whatever to the contents of the _patta_ of which this was a certified copy, this might well indicate somebody's quick assessment of the revenue that was to be levied on the grant mentioned in the _patta_, now that decision to that effect had been taken by the British. We find Damodar depositing, tentatively, the amount of Rs. 13 as revenue in the middle of July, 1846. This is, as can be seen, very close to the amount mentioned on this copy. However, a question which arises is that if copies of the original _pattas_ were being prepared and supplied to owners of land, why are there no copies of other _pattas_ which were originally in the possessions of the painters? To this there is no easy answer.

Original _pattas_ or not, the value of these documents still remains. Quite a large number of points emerge from the study of these, for each of them has something to contribute to our understanding of the total situation with regard to art and patronage and land-grants in the hills etc. However, perhaps the points will be best made by each document itself when it is translated and annotated later. Here, some use might be served by a tabulated statement which gives briefly the facts of each document and an indication of what it contains.

ABSTRACT OF THE DOCUMENTS

No.	Date	Issuing authority	Place of issue	Nature	Grantee	Contents
I	31 Asuj 1882 (1825)	Maharaja Ranjit Singh	Ram Bagh (Amritsar)	Parwana	Nikka	Informing the Kardar of Rihlu that land worth Rs. 125/- per annum has been granted, as of old, to the painter Nikka according to the recommendation of Sardar Budh Singh. This land is to be free of the imposition of kar and begar etc.
II	23 Magh (1825)	(Raja Dhyan Singh) (Sahi in Takri)	?	Parwana	Nikka	Asking Ganda Mal, Kardar of Rihlu, to hand over land in full measure as granted by the Huzur to Nikka. Says that the nazrana from the grantee should not be detained there. (No indication of the value of land and size of holding.)
III	9 Magh 1893 (=1836) 11 June 1846	Original Maharaja Ranjit Singh copy: Agent of the Governor General	?	Copy of Patta of the Maharaja, duly certified	Gokal	Asking the amils of Haripur and Guler not to interfere with the jagir land of Rs. 1oo/- per annum granted to the painter Gokal. Mentions that the signatures of Sardar Lehna Singh Sandhanwalia be obtained.
IV	23 Sawan 1894 (1837)	?	Lahore	Parwana	Gokal	Asking Kahan Singh Kang(?) to hand over land to the painter Gokal, servant of Sardar Attar Singh, as per the parwana of the Sarkar.

No.	Date	Issuing authority	Place of issue	Nature	Grantee	Contents
V	25 Sawan 1894(?) (1837)	Ajit Singh	?	*Parwana*	Gokal	Asking Lala Kahan Singh to hand over good land to Gokal as per the *parwana* of Khalsa Jio and Raja *Sahib* (Dhian Singh), regarding *muafi* of land to him.
VI	25 Asuj 1897	Ajit Singh Sandhanwalia	Drang (Mandi Hills)	*Parwana*	Gokal	Ordering Missar Mayya Das to see to it that no interference is offered to the painter Gokal in the enjoyment of his *jagir* in *taaluqa* Ramgarh. No *tambul* or *bhati* etc. should be levied upon him.
VII	?	?	?	Letter	Chhajju and Harkhu	Asking Sardar Lehna Singh (Majithia?) to intervene in the matter of getting the release of Chhajju, the painter, who has been falsely accused of murder. Stating that Harkhu is in the employment of the Khalsa Jio and both are deserving of favourable consideration.
VIII	18 Maghar 1898 (1841)	Maharaja Sher Singh	Ram Bagh (Amritsar)	*Parwana*	Gokal	Informing Sardar Lehna Singh Majithia that *jagir* valued at Rs. 225/- per *annum* has been conferred upon the painter Gokal in the *taaluqas* of Rihlu and Haripur. The painter was formerly in the employment of the Sandhanwalia Sardars.

No.	Date	Issuing authority	Place of issue	Nature	Grantee	Contents
IX	27 Maghar 1898 (1841)	Bawa Lachhman Singh	?	Parwana	Gokal	Asking Chaudhari Chuhar to allow the jagir of Rs. 225/- per annum as the share of Gokal to remain with him in the taaluqas of Rihlu and Haripur as granted in muafi by the Sarkar.
X	27 Maghar 1898 (1841)	Bawa Lachhman Singh	?	Parwana	Gokal	Asking Bhagat Boghu Shah to allow the jagir worth Rs. 225/- per annum in the taaluqas of Rihlu and Haripur to remain in the possession of the painter Gokal, as per the parwana of the Sarkar.
XI	2o Asuj 1899 (1842)	Lehna Singh Majithia	Lahore	Parwana	Harkhu	Asking Bhagat Boghu Shah to give the (cash) grant of Rs. 2oo/- per annum to the painter Harkhu in place of the painter Fauju who used to receive it from the late Raja Sahib (Sansar Chand?).
XII	?	?	?	Parwana	Chhajju and Gokal	Asking Chhajju to share the land (and its produce) worth Rs. 225/- per annum, already in his possession, with the painter Gokal, in equal measure.
XIII	?	Narayan Chaudhry	?	Rugga'	Chhajju	Note to Lala Sohna Mal asking him to help Chhajju get his salary etc. from the toshakhana.

No.	Date	Issuing authority	Place of issue	Nature	Grantee	Contents
XIV	1o Jeth 19oo (1843)	Sher Singh	?	Order of appointment	Gokal	Asking the mutasaddis of the Daftar-i-Mualla to enter the name of Gokal in the records as being in the employment of Sarkar on terms indicated.
XV	16 Magh 19o2	Ranjodh Singh	The Talwan crossing	Parwana	Gokal	Asking Wazir Karam Singh to treat the muafi of Rs. 1oo/- in the name of Gokal in taaluqa Haripur as duly confirmed. This is in addition to the conferment of Rs. 5o/- on Chhajju.
XVI	8 July 1846	Munshi (Sayyad?) Hadi Hussain Khan	?	Receipt	Damodar	Receipt of the amount of Rs. 13/- as land revenue from Damodar. (No mention of crop etc.)
XVII	1o Sept. 1846	Sayyad Hadi Hussain Khan	?	Receipt	Damodar	Receipt of the amount of Rs. 15/6/6 as revenue on the Rabi' crop of 19o3 on land now resumed. (No mention of instalment).
XVIII	1 Nov. 1846	Munshi Hadi Hussain Khan	?	Receipt	Damodar	Receipt for land revenue of the amount of Rs. 42/2/= from Damodar for the instalment due in November 1846, for the Kharif crop.
XIX	27 Jan. 1847	Munshi Hadi Hussain Khan	?	Receipt	Damodar	Receipt of Rs. 43/1/6 as revenue for the Kharif crop of 19o3: instalment due in January 1847.
XX	?	Saudagar	?	Wajib-ul-arz	Saudagar	Petition to the Maharani (of Chamba?) that his salary may be raised from Rs. 15/- per mensem that he now gets. This money is inadequate since the late Maharaja used to give the painter much more besides the cash pay.

VI The Questions

There is a great deal of hard, factual information that these documents yield. Our picture of what was happening at the Lahore Court in the 19th century in the matter of patronage of art assumes much more fullness after a study of these than before. But whole series of questions remain: some of them suggested by the evidence of these documents themselves, others inadequately answered by them. What, for instance, one would have liked to know, was the precise nature of the relationship between these patrons and painters? How did they come together? Did the patrons substantially affect the style of work being done for them? Did the painters, in turn, influence the taste of their patrons? Was there a discussion of the points of a painting between them? Or of themes? Was the painter free to do what he wished? Did the patron specify his wishes? How did he see the work of these painters as against those of others? Again: what was the degree of mobility that the painter possessed? Was the decision to shift from one patron to another his own? Was economic gain a major motive with him? Did he feel fulfilled in working for patrons who belonged to a different cultural group and had a different life-style?

To these and other questions, as has been pointed out before, there are no answers in these documents. Nor is there any but the most indirect indication herein of the quality of work being done by these painters. A question that could be usefully speculated on, however, is the range of themes that these painters treated of in their work. The view that is commonly taken, of course, is that 'painting in the Punjab' means little else than 'Sikh Painting', and Sikh painting, as W.G. Archer sees it, is "chiefly an art of portraiture".[112] It is possible to see why portraiture is emphasized as "a typical expression" of Sikh painting by nearly everyone. For one thing, a large number of portraits are historically interesting, can obviously be seen as 'Sikh' because of the persons that figure in them, and are thus easier to place in a distinct category. For another, it is possible to tie up the Sikh preference for pageantry and colour with some of the more flamboyant portraits. But then one can be sure that much more than portraiture was being done for these very Sikh patrons in the Punjab, and in a style that could still be distinctly seen as Pahari. Would one say then that the work of the same painters for the same set of patrons was in part 'Sikh' and in part 'Pahari' or 'Punjabi'? Would that not be an artificial distinction to make, a position difficult to take?

Possibly too little attention has gone to work other than portraiture done in the Punjab in the nineteenth century. The very painters that we have seen as active in the Punjab in these documents must have been kept busy by many more things that portraits of their patrons or of other personalities at the Court. There must have been the recognizably 'Sikh' subjects such as sets of 'portraits' of the Sikh Gurus to which Mr. Archer draws attention early in his work. These must have been turned out in large numbers, and not for Sikh patrons alone. Then there is the considerable body of work which is by now beginning to receive attention: illustration to the Janam Sakhis.[113] Many of these were produced in the standard 'Kashmiri' style which appears so ubiquitously in the Punjab, but we know also of many which are clearly the work of Pahari artists. This work has survived both in the form of finished paintings inserted inside bound manuscripts of the text and in the form of very accomplished drawings. The extensive set of drawings of one Janam Sakhi which is in the Chandigarh Museum,[114] thus, is fairly clearly the work of a member of the Nainsukh family as is the painted Janam Sakhi in the possession of Rao Uttam Singh of Sangrur.[115]

It is not unlikely again that some of the artists in the Punjab were kept engaged working on those murals of which we hear a great deal in the accounts of the travellers and contemporary accounts. Many of the murals that have survived are of the late 19th century, but earlier murals descended clearly from the Pahari tradition from the hills are not unknown. The themes of Nayakas and Nayikas and erotic scenes and 'mythological' subjects that find such detailed mention in an account, for instance, like that of Lieutenant Barr[116] are also indicative of the connection of these murals with the Pahari work of the 18th century with which we are so familiar.

But it is not difficult to envisage even more than this being done by the painters for their Sikh patrons. The themes that we roughly call 'Hindu' or 'Rajput' could not have been treated all in the hills for Hindu patrons, for we have to see the first half of the 19th century in its own terms. A sharp distinction between Hindus and Sikhs, or Hindu themes and Sikh themes, perhaps did not apply at that point of time and belongs almost certainly to a much later period. The homage that Maharaja Ranjit Singh offered again and again at 'Hindu' sacred places like Kangra and Jwalamukhi in the hills,[117] cannot simply have been an act of prudence in politics. Ranjit Singh's father had been to Jwalamukhi on a pilgrimage, as had been his grandfather, and they had duly entered their names in the registers of the pandas there.[118] Ranjit Singh, while a good Sikh himself, paid nonetheless sincere attention to places connected with the Hindus, and gave generous grants. When we look at the spirit of the times, then, a statement such as Lehna Singh Majithia wishing to leave the Punjab in 1844 to go on a long 'pilgrimage to Haridwar or Benares' comes as completely natural. There is no surprise about this, nothing unusual. These are Hindu places of pilgrimage which it would be difficult to associate with the Sikhs today, but in the first half of the 19th century, for the Sikhs to go on pilgrimage to these places was perhaps not abnormal. If one remembers this, it becomes possible to visualise a situation in which we see a large number of so-called Hindu or Rajput paintings being acutally executed in the plains of the Punjab for different patrons, both Hindu and Sikh. It is not without interest in this context to recall that there are several paintings of the well-known 'Kangra' sets such as the _Gita Govinda_ which have at their backs not only inscribed texts in Sanskrit but also their rendering in Punjabi. While it is entirely possible that paintings of these sets might have passed into the hands of Sikh or Punjabi owners _after_ they had been executed in the hills for a prince there, the possibility that some of these or similar works were commissioned by Sikh patrons for themselves cannot be at once ruled out. The fairly extensive _Rasikapriya_ set dealing with Krishna and Radha themes which comes from the second half of the 19th century and belonged to the Sikh ruling house of Kapurthala[119] comes as no surprise in this situation, nor do the Shish Mahal frescoes from the Sikh court of Patiala[120] which treat of subjects from the _Satsai_ of Bihari, or the _Kavipriya_ of Keshavadasa, or the _avataras_ of Vishnu and the _Virata Rupa_ of Krishna.

Perhaps it is both possible and necessary then for us to see 'Sikh Painting' in a different light than we have been doing till now.

NOTES

1 The village of Gaggal is technically a <u>tika</u> of the <u>mauza</u> of Rajol, in the tahsil of Kangrā in the district of that very name. The family of artists residing here is known to art historians chiefly as the "artist family of Rajol". For a discussion of the genealogy of this family, see B.N. Goswamy, "The artist family of Rajol: New Light on an old Problem", <u>Roopalekha</u>, vol. XXXV.

2 For the latest discussion on Nainsukh, see W.G. Archer, <u>Indian Paintings from the Punjab Hills</u>, (London 1973), vol. I, pp 183-2o8. The literature on Nainsukh is by now considerable, for he is one of the most engaging figures in the history of Pahaṛī Painting. See, thus, K. Khandalavala, "Balvant Singh of Jammu - a Patron of Pahari Painting", Bul. <u>Prince of Wales Museum,</u> 1951-52, no. 2; B.N. Goswamy, "Pahaṛī Painting; The Family as the Basis of Style", <u>Mārg</u>, Sept.1968.

3 I wish to express here my deep gratitude to Srī Chandu Lal and the members of his family as also to the family of Srī Bhupindar Prakash Raina who have given me generously of their valuable time and information.

4 This appears to have been the traditional way in which valuable papers used to be kept. The <u>pandas</u> or priests at many centres of pilgrimage keep their <u>sanads</u> received from their powerful clients in this manner. If occasionally a scorpion comes crawling out of one such bamboo tube, one takes it, I suppose, as a professional hazard!

5 The use of Persian in the government and administration not only of Mahārāja Ranjīt Singh, but also by his Sikh predeccessors in the Punjab, is something to which we are by now used. For a series of Sikh documents in Persian, see B.N. Goswamy and J.S. Grewal, <u>The Mughal and Sikh rulers and the Vaishnavas of Pindori</u>, (Simla, 1969) (Hereinafter referred to as <u>The Pindori Documents</u>). As pointed out by us earlier, Ranjīt Singh's attitude towards Persian is extremely interesting. The poet Ahmad yar, author of the <u>Shah nama-i-Ranjit Singh</u>, desired to write his work in the Punjabi language, but the Mahārāja ordered that it should be composed in Persian, for it was the "language prized by the learned".

6 This is a point with which anyone who has worked on documents of this sort would be only too familiar. The <u>shikasteh</u> is not the most friendly of scripts and presents sometimes almost insurmountable difficulties. The documents from the 16th century employ <u>nastālīq</u> of the most elegant kind and it is much later perhaps that the use of <u>shikasteh</u> became current in the administrative documents.

7 "A mandate,command order or royal patent" (Steingass, *Persian-English Dictionary*). For examples of some Moghul *farmans* that we found in the course of our field-work in the Punjab, see B.N.Goswamy and J.S. Grewal, *The Mughals and the Jogis of Jakhbar*, (Simla 1967) (Hereinafter referred to as *The Jakhbar Documents*).

8 Dr. Ifran Habīb, in his splendid work, *The Agrarian system of Mughal India* (London 1966), p. 23o, points out that the *pattā* may originally have been the written document mentioned by Abu'l Fazl which was given to each individual cultivator after his revenue demand had been determined. The word, however, came later to be used in a much looser sense and signified almost any official or semi-official document recording any grant etc.

9 Steingass defines a parwānā as: "a royal patent or diploma; a grant or letter under the great seal from any man in power; a pass, licence, leave, permit, command, precept, warrant, written order or commission". In popular usage, a parwānā occupies probably a lower status than a *pattā* or *farmān*, both of which possess a more formal character. In these documents the words *parwānā-i-wālā* are often used to describe them.

1o While one is familiar with stray documents that yield information of value from time to time, a whole group of documents of this order is not perhaps known. Even for the Mughal period, for which our documentation is thus far the best, a body of evidence such as this is unfortunately not known.

11 See, thus, B.N. Goswamy, "The family as the Basis of style &c.". *Mārg*, Sept. 1968; Archer, *Indian Paintings from the Punjab Hills*. Practically every art historian concerned with Paharī Painting has taken this family into account.

12 The style that is referred to as the style of this family of artists is generally described as "Kangra" by scholars. To this "Kangra" style, of course, several studies and monographs have been devoted. The works, thus, of M.S. Randhawa, Karl Khandalavala and W.G. Archer are only too well known to students of the subject.

13 For a reconstruction of the genealogical table of this family, going back to *Data* whose name occurs in a family tree mentioned by Nainsukh in his own hand, see B.N. Goswamy, "The Family as the Basis of style &c.".

14 This portrait is in the Chandigarh Museum. For a reproduction of it, see *ibid*,, p. 25, no. 1.

15 The portrait of Mānaku is also in the Chandigarh Museum, but the whereabouts of that of Nainsukh, which was once in the Tagore Collection, are not now known. For reproduction of these, see *ibid*,,

15 cont.
p. 25, nos. 2 and 3.

16 For a discussion of the work of this family of artists and for reproduction of portraits of the four sons of Nainsukh, see *ibid.*, p. 25, nos. 4 to 7 and pp. 31 to 57.

17 All the records relating to this family that have so far come to light point to the fact that the family sees Guler as its native place of origin. If an entry of A.D. 1736 in the records of the priests gives Guler as the only place connected with the family, it is indication enough that the family must have been settled there for at least two to three generations before that time. The painters are often referred to as "Guleria chitreras", pointing once again to their Guler origin.

18 For the most recent discussion of the paintings of Balvant Singh, see Archer, *Indian Paintings from the Punjab Hills*, pp. 194-2o8. It may be mentioned that Mr. Archer thinks of Balvant Singh as a Prince from Jammu whereas I speak of him as belonging to the Jasrota royal house, because that is where my evidence leads me. This disagreement does not of course, fortunately, affect the quality of these remarkable studies!

19 See B.N. Goswamy, "A painter's letter to His Royal Patron: An old Takrī document", *J. of the Am.Or.Soc.*, vol. 86, no. 2. This rather singular document is in the possession of Srī Jagannath Pahda of Basohli through whose kind courtesy I was able to have access to it.

2o For a discussion of the oral and documentary evidence on this point, see B.N. Goswamy, "Painting in Chamba: A study of new documents", *Asian Review/ Art and Letters* (London), vol. II, no. 1.

21 According to Srī Chandulal, this silver plate was in the family till not very long ago and belonged to one of his collaterals to whose share it fell as a part of the family property when it was divided. I have unfortunately not been able to trace the plate and it is not unlikely that it has been sold away or used.

22 For a detailed reproduction of this 'magic diagram', see B.N. Goswamy, "Of Patronage and Pahari Painters", in P. Pal (ed.), *Aspects of Indian Art* (Los Angeles. 1972). The original list of names of states and patrons published by me in *Mārg*, Sept. 1968, was imperfect, because of a poor photograph. All the entries have now been read and published in the more recent article.

23 Jai Singh was one of the most important of the Sikh chiefs of the 18th century and struck a seal in his own name which is to be found in some of *The Pindori Documents* (nos.XXIV, XXV). Jai Singh operated

23 cont.

from the Batala-Mukerian area in the foothills but considerably expanded his influence and domains. For details of the career of this rather remarkable figure, see H.R. Gupta, History of the Sikhs, I, pp. 51-52, 95, 99, 127; III, pp. 3-4, 22, 23, 25, 26-27, 34-4o, 41, 43, 44.

24 For some documents issued by, and in the name of, Gurbaksh Singh, see The Pindori Documents, nos. XXIX - XXXIV. Gurbaksh Singh predeceased his father and was killed in a battle (of which we have a touching account) with Sardar Jassa Singh Ramgarhia.

25 Like Jai Singh, Jassa Singh was a Sikh Chief of great importance in the second half of the 18th century and operated as much in the plains of the Punjab close to the hills as in some of the Hill states themselves. As his full name indicates, he was the head of the Ramgarhia misl.

26 The settlement reports bear the names of these years even though it must be remembered that the work preparatory to the settlements was done in the years preceding. The entries in the records of the report of 1868 were actually made sometimes in 1865-66.

27 The reason why the date of the death of Nikka is given as "c. A.D. 1833" is that the record of the priests mentions this particular date but, as was the practice in the hills, the ashes of dead persons were sometimes kept stored and taken to Haridwar for immersion into the river only when a group formed to proceed on that long pilgrimage. The death of Nikka could thus have occurred either in that year itself or, at a guess, in the year or two preceeding it.

28 The whole question of the identification of styles of Pahari paintings on the basis of state names is somewhat problematic and open to revision. I have considered the possibility of naming styles after families of artists in my "The Family as the Basis of style etc.". The most recent work of Dr. Archer describes the painting of different areas not as paintings of that school, but executed in those centres. Thus, "Painting in Guler", "Painting in Kangra", etc. The term Kangra in particular is perhaps the best known as a description of a style of great luxuriance and refinement and is most often almost equated with Pahari painting itself.

29 Several writers have had to take the phenomenon of Sikh painting into account, but do not seem to do it with any marked pleasure considering the summary manner in which it has so far been dismissed and the somewhat patronizing or contemptuous tone adopted towards it. Most often, this attitude has been sought to be justified because, as the last of the phase of "Kangra" painting, it stands in

29 cont.
marked contrast to the reticence and the refinement of the best work of that "school".

3o <u>Paintings of the Sikhs</u>, (London 1966).

31 <u>Ibid.</u>, p. 18.

32 Chandigarh Museum, no. 25o . The persons in this painting are identified in a long inscription which seems to tally perfectly with the appearances of these persons, which are known to us from other portraits.

33 Reproduced, Archer, <u>Indian Paintings from the Punjab Hills</u>, vol.II, Guler 51. This painting is now in the Victoria & Albert Museum, French collection, I.S. 128-1955.

34 Chandigarh Museum.

35 No. 1948-1o-9-o131. This is really a drawing which is very faintly tinted in mauve and is obviously from a sketch book. Inscriptions identifying Jassa Singh appear on this both in English and in Nāgarī.

36 This painting bears no. 17-27o8. Unfortunately all the figures are difficult to identify because of lack of inscriptions. The painting is in the style that we associate with so many of the Darbar scenes from the court of Sansar Chand.

37 For an account of the role played by these Sikh chiefs in the developments in the hills, see J. Hutchison and J. Ph. Vogel, <u>History of the Punjab Hill States</u>, (Lahore 1933), vols. I and II.

38 See Archer, <u>Paintings of the Sikhs</u>, pp. 6o-62. Both Kehar Singh and Kapur Singh are briefly studied by M.S. Randhawa in <u>Chhavi</u>, (Golden Jubilee Volume, Bharat Kala Bhavan, Banaras 1971), in his article, "Two Panjabi Artists of the nineteenth century - Kehar Singh and Kapur Singh", pp. 67-69. A number of paintings by Kapur Singh showed up at Maggs Brothers in London some years ago.

39 For a full reproduction of this entry in the <u>bahi</u> of the pandas of Haridwar, see B.N. Goswamy, "The Family as the Basis of style etc."

4o No. 1922-12-14-o1. Devi Ditta appears in that painting between 3o and 35 years of age, wearing a yellow turban, a white Jama with light green border and a pointed beard. The inscriptions that identify both Dhyan Singh and Devi Ditta are in Nāgarī and Persian scripts. For other portraits of Raja Dhyan Singh, see Archer, <u>Paintings of the Sikhs</u>,nos. 24-33, 35, etc.

41 <u>Handbook of the Manufactures and Arts of the Punjab</u>, (Lahore 1872), p. 355. Baden Powell speaks of the "remarkable clearness of tone, and delicacy of handling" in Purkhu's work.

42 This is a little village which lay across the khad which separated the domains of Sansar Chand from those of the Sikhs after they occupied the Kangra Fort in 1809. Samloti is a village of no consequence other than that it was a place where this family and other families of artists were settled by Sansar Chand.

43 The family table available with the family of Srī Gulabu Ram, a descendant of Purkhu, mentions that Purkhu's father was Dhumun, a fact confirmed by the settlement record of the village from the year 1868.

44 This sketch was seen by me in 1964 and, even though the entire inscription could not be read, the fact that it is a note mentioning all the three brothers emerged clearly.

45 The Real Ranjit Singh, (Karachi, 1965), p. 121. A number of paintings are also reproduced in this book.

46 See H. Goetz, "Some Portraits of the Pahari School in Dutch collections", JISOA, vol. I, no. 2. A long verse in Hindī is at the back of this painting and Dr. Goetz provides a full translation, in which the different figures are identified. The description, however, as "King Visava Singh" is not really accurate for the word "Maharaj" which means to have been used in the original Hindī is clearly loosely employed and does not literally mean a king. As we shall see later, the principal figure may be none other than one of the Sandhanwalia brothers.

47 For a full bibliography, see Archer, Paintings of the Sikhs. A work like Khushwant Singh's A History of the Sikhs, (Princeton 1966), reconstructs with great vividness the history of the Sikh kingdom. As a contemporary account Sohanlal's Umdat-ut-Tawarikh, (translated by V.S. Suri) is invaluable because of the atmosphere and the flavour of the period that it is able to convey.

48 It is not only for the European visitors, some of whom were keen on drawing, that Ranjit Singh must have sat. Despite the interesting stories about his reluctance in the matter due to his pock-marked and one-eyed face, it is almost certain that likenesses of his from life were taken by Indian painters.

49 The interest shown by the European visitors in Indian miniatures was not in-considerable: it is the respect for these which was so slight in their case. One comes upon an occasional word of praise for a particular aspect of these paintings, such as the line, but the work as a whole is really poorly regarded.

50 For an account of the Sandhanwalias, see Lepel Griffin, History of the Punjab Chiefs, (Lahore, 1865), pp. 11-28. A family tree of the Sandhanwalias is appended, tracing their ancestry back to Buddha

50 cont.
Singh, who was great-great-grandfather of Maharaja Ranjit Singh. Also see, H.R. Gupta, Punjab on the Eve of First Sikh War, (Hoshiarpur 1956), pp. 17-18.

51 Umdat-ut-Tawarikh, (edited by V.S. Suri), III, pp. 315-316.

52 It needs to be mentioned as a word of caution in the matter of accepting the strings of high-sounding titles, however, that they were conferred rather generously and did not often mean too much. "Ujjal didar, nirmal budh" are epithets that were indeed employed with such great frequency that they must have lost all meaning.

53 For the Majithias, see Griffin, op.cit., pp. 83-91. Mr. Archer (Paintings of the Sikhs), pp. 18-22, sees both the Majithias, father and son as almost pivotal figures in the development of Sikh painting by Pahari Painters. The two portraits that he believes possibly to represent Desa Singh and Lehna Singh (figs. 1o and 36) raise serious question. We have a portrait of Lehna Singh Majithia in the Chandigarh Museum which is very different from that taken by Mr. Archer to be possibly that of Lehna Singh.

54 This painting was reproduced in V.C. Ohri, "Four important inscriptions on Pahari paintings", Lalit Kala, no. 11. For a discussion of the inscription on the painting, see B.N. Goswamy, "Painting in Chamba etc.", Lalit Kala, no. 15.

55 For the details of the developments at this point of time, see Gazetteer of the Kangra district, 1883-84 and in Hutchison and Vogel, vol. I.

56 See, thus, Gazetteer of the Kangra district, vol. I, 1883-84, pp. 218-222.

57 Although no specific instances can be cited out of hand, it is easy to see people whose loyalty to the new regime was not complete being out of favour and thus losing whatever jāgīrs or other grants they held from the former rulers. On the other hand, new jāgīrs must have been created in large numbers for the purpose of bringing into being new and vested interests that supported the new rule. The word jāgīr is being used here in the loose sense in which it is often found in popular usage and not solely in the sense of "... an assignment of the government share of the produce of a large tract of country to an individual; a possession in land granted either in perpetuity or for life as a reward for services or as a fee" (Steingass, Persian-English Dictionary). For a full discussion of the whole question of jāgīrs, see Irfan Habib, pp. 257-297.

58 Wilson, A Glossary of Judicial and Revenue terms, etc., (London 1855), pp. 224-225, mentions, among varieties of jāgīrs, a khidmati

58 cont.
jāgīr which is obviously assignment of land to village servants and officers against payment of salaries. Also see, Irfan Habib, pp. 3o7-3o8, 316.

59 Muāfī is a word which one comes upon often and is to be understood as something that is "exempt from the payment of rent or tax etc." (Steingass). Wilson's Glossary (p. 346) describes it as "a grant of land free of assessment", and adds: "the word is in common use to signify exempt or free from duty or tax, as lands, goods, etc.".

6o See Lepel Griffin, pp. 11-28, for the relationship between the Sandhanwalias and the Maharaja.

61 At an early point of time the Sandhanwalias received jāgīrs worth Rupees 1,8o,ooo from the Maharaja in the ilāqās of Saho, Talwan etc. Most of theses jāgīrs were confiscated later by the orders of Hira Singh; the British later restored some of these to Sardar Shamsher Singh in the Raja Sansi area.

62 The Pahari says: "jeena, pahāre dā jeenā" meaning: "life has meaning only in the hills".

63 It may seem likely that the references to "grants from previous rules" which we find so often in The Jakhbar Documents and in The Pindori Documents were almost a formula repeated as a matter of course from grant to grant, but this was not really the case in fact, because new grants were always specifically indicated to be new. It is possible that the reference in this document is to grants by Rajput Chiefs before the Sikh rule, but it is also conceivable that a grant by Ranjit Singh himself of an earlier date is being alluded to here.

64 For examples of these see The Jakhbar Documents, no II and III. The words used for the detailed endorsements there are sharah-i-taliqah.

65 For the multifarious duties of the kārdārs who were more than simply revenue collectors, see Umdat-ut-Tawarikh, III, pp. 4, 56, 75, 8o, 93, 132, 141, 146, 177, 183-84, 2o3, 223, 241, 255, etc. Also see, Gazetteer of the Kangra District, vol. I, 1883-84, p. 219. The judgement of this work on the kārdārs is stern: their corruption and dishonesty lead to the comment that "a kārdār was an offender almost beyond the hope of pardon".

66 See, thus, B.N. Goswamy, "Family as the Basis of Style", Mārg, Sept. 1968, for fuller details of these entries.

67 Ajit Singh was the son of Wasawa Singh and played a prominent role in the events after the death of the great Maharaja. A portrait of

67 cont.
Ajit Singh is reproduced in Archer, <u>Paintings of the Sikhs</u>, fig. 83.

68 The <u>Gazetteer of the Kangra District</u>, vol. I, 1883-84, p. 5o, has this on the <u>taaluqa</u>: "In every pargana is comprised a number of minor subdivisions called <u>talukas</u>. These <u>talukas</u> are of very ancient origin contemporaneous probably with the first occupation of the hills. They all bear distinctive names and their boundaries usually follow the natural variations of the country". In the plains also, of course, the <u>taaluqa</u> as an administrative subdivision was known. When the <u>Gazetteer of the Kangra District</u> of 1883-84 was compiled, the district of Kangra had 38 <u>taaluqas</u> which were grouped into four <u>tahsīls</u>.

69 Haripur was the principal town of the ancient principality of Guler, but with the disappearance of the rule of the Rajas after the take-over, first by the Sikhs and then by the British, Haripur-Guler became first a <u>tahsil</u> and then a <u>taaluqa</u> in the tahsil of Dehra in the Kangra District. See ibid., pp. 7, 49.

7o The <u>taaluqa</u> of Rihlu has a great deal of history attaching to it, for it was the bone of contention between the neighbouring states of Kangra and Chamba. It was the object of much dispute for the obvious reasons of its great fertility. Tradition has it that when the Mughals conquered Kangra, it was this <u>taaluqa</u>, "which equalled in richness the most eligible district in the hills", which alone was annexed as an imperial appanage. It was over the retention of Rihlu by Chamba against Kangra that Raj Singh died fighting Sansar Chand in 1794. See, thus, <u>Gazetteer of the Kangra District</u>, 1883-84, p. 44.

71 The <u>khālisa</u> comprised "the lands and sources of revenue reserved for the imperial treasury" in Mughal India. See, Irfan Habib, p. 259. The idea of the <u>khālisa</u> lands continues almost unchanged in the Sikh period also; but the word has, of course, to be distinguished carefully from <u>khālsā</u> which signifies the Sikh community in general, and from <u>khālsā-Jio</u> which is used often to describe the ruler as in <u>The Pindori Documents</u>, much the same as in the documents treated of here.

72 The word used is <u>mulāzim</u> which literally means "a servant". This is a description which theoretically applies to virtually everyone below the ruler, but perhaps the sense in which it is used for a painter is different than when it would be used in connection with a high official like a minister. For the painters the word <u>chākar</u> also was employed which has the same meaning. A leaf from a sketch book in the Chandigarh Museum has little portrait heads of the artists Arjan, Ruldu and Kanchanu who are all described as <u>mulāzims</u>

72 cont.
of the Jammu Maharaja.

73 The taaluqa of Ramgarh was, after 1846, in the tahsil of Haripur at first, but was later transferred to the jurisdiction of the Kangra tahsil (Gazetteer of the Kangra District, 1883-84, p. 49). Geographically it is separated only by a stream from the neighbouring taaluqa of Rihlu.

74 Apparently, an official attached to the governor of the hills, Sardar Lehna Singh. The Umdat-ut-Tawarikh, vol. IV, p. 224, mentions a "Baba" Lachhman Singh to whom instructions are issued by Maharaja Sher Singh to look after "Clerk Sahib" who was to pass through those territories. He is mentioned again in the Newsletter of 19th August 1844 from Lahore as a "confidential servant" of Sardar Ranjodh Singh Majithia, half-brother of Lehna Singh, who took over the affairs of the hills for a short while. See H.R. Gupta, Punjab on the eve of the First Sikh War, p. 278.

75 The Gazetteer of the Kangra District, 1883-84, p. 218, has this to say on Lehna Singh: "Sardar Lehna Singh enjoys a good reputation in the hills; he was a mild and lenient governor; his periodical visits were not made a pretence for oppressing and plundering the people; he maintained a friendly intercourse with the deposed hill chiefs, and contributed by his conciliatory manners to alleviate their fallen position. At the same time he is held in favourable recollection by the peasantry. His assessments were moderate for a native system, and although he did not possess that force of character to keep his agents under proper control, yet he never himself oppressed, nor willingly countenanced oppression in others." Also see, Lepel Griffin, pp. 83-91. It is not certain that Harkhu was attached by Lehna Singh to himself. He might only have been carrying out orders from above.

76 Dr. Irfan Habib (p. 298) identifies āimma with madad-i-ma'āsh grants. The word, according to him, was a "plural of Īmām, literally meaning (village) leader, but by a linguistic corruption, applied to the land covered by the grants". As pointed out in The Jakhbar Documents (pp. 21-22, 46) and in The Pindori Documents (pp. 81 etc.), the aimma was by no means limited to grants given to Muslims, as often supposed. The use of the word here is certainly of interest.

77 A mutasaddi is defined by Steingass as: "any inferior officer of Government, a clerk, accountant". Also see, Irfan Habib, p. 287 and The Jakhbar Documents, p. 135.

78 Literally, "the exalted office". Under the Sikh regime, this office apparently was well organised and treated of matters specifically allotted to it. Quite obviously records of enrolment into royal ser-

78 cont.
vice were maintained in this office.

79 There is a great deal of mention of this move of Lehna Singh who, taking the developments of 1843-44 to be "a cause of everlasting misfortune... to stay any more in the metropolis of Lahore took leave from Raja Hira Singh and left for Ganga Ji". Umdat-ut-Tawarikh, vol. IV, p. 277. Lepel Griffin, p. 91, passes a stern judgement on Lehna Singh on this point who, he says, was "ever-ready, at the approach of danger, to run off to Haridwar to bathe or to Benares to feed a crowd of hungry Brahmans". We know that Pandit Jalla was unhappy at Lehna Singh's "slipping away", as it were.

8o Ranjodh Singh took over when Lehna Singh left on his pilgrimage and it was he who delivered the fiscal papers of the Kangra territory to the Commissioner after the cession of the hills to the British in March 1846. See Gazetteer of the Kangra District, 1883-84, p. 221.

81 The amount of correspondence on jāgīrs is considerable. The files are among the Foreign, Political Consultations of the year 1846-47 in the National Archives. One of the more detailed ones is in Consultation numbers 2185-2197 dated 31.12.1847.

82 In a note dated November 16, 1846, Sir John Lawrence made a detailed recommendation to the Governor General regarding the jāgīr cases and the Governor General's reply agrees that "to settle matters once for all is desirable". Then it proceeds to lay down general principles and attaches various statements etc. See, Foreign, Political Consultation, 2185-2197, dated 31.12.1847.

83 The branch of Chhajju must have, likewise, done the same but the documents pertaining to that branch are no longer in the present collection. It might be mentioned that Gokal's ashes were taken to Haridwar in S. 19o4 (A.D. 1846/47).

84 Literally, a superscription that appears on the top of a document. The Sar-i-nāmah appears on practically all documents from the early time, Hindu, Muslim, Sikh. The most commonly employed sar-i-nāmah on Persian documents of the Muslim period, in its abbreviated form, appears as the letter alif. This, in the case of Muslim documents, easily can be seen to stand for Allāh-u-Akbar and is retained on Hindu documents, where it is ingeniously turned to signify perhaps Omkār and on Sikh documents to signify Akāl Purkh. See, The Jakhbar Documents and The Pindori Documents for examples.

85 This has received considerable and detailed attention in recent years. The name obviously comes from the East-India Company for the servants of which these paintings were often produced to order. See for details the work of Mrs. Mildred Archer, who has produced some

85 cont.
remarkably well-documented works, such as Company Drawings in the India Office Library, (London 1972).

86 See, B.N. Goswamy, "Pahari Painting; The Family as the Basis of style", Mārg, Sept. 1968, pp. 3o-31. The date of Devi Ditta's migration from Lahore to Patiala is not precisely indicated. An unusually large painting showing a court procession, possibly of Raja Mahendar Singh, is in the Museum in the Shish Mahal Palace at Patiala.

87 Biba belongs to the family to which the painter Ghathu Ram of Guler also belonged. The information about his working at Patiala came from Lachhman Das of Guler, the last descendant of this family, who died a few years ago.

88 The name of this painter appears in an inscription in Persian below a painting of Guru Govind Singh which was formerly in the collection of Sri Ram Ji Das of Patiala. The name of the patron to whom this painting was presented, Bhai Gurmukh Singh, also appears in the inscription.

89 For a discussion of these frescoes, see, Karuna Goswamy, "The frescoes in the Shish Mahal Palace at Patiala", Rooplekha, vol. 38, nos. 1/2. It appears that a family of artists from Alwar or Jaipur was engaged in this work also.

9o A visit of Saudagar to Haridwar is recorded in the year 1866 and another again in 1871. The second entry mentions Saudagar as "employed in Tehri (Garhwal)". See B.N. Goswamy, "Pahari Painting; Family as the Basis of style", p. 3o.

91 This letter is reproduced in B.N. Goswamy, "A Painter's letter to his Royal Patron: An Old Takri Document", J. American Oriental Society, vol. 86, no. 2, April-June 1966. Among the other things that Shiba says, is this outspoken passage: "The thing that matters is one's own self (literally, "belly"). All rights or wrongs that anyone does, he does for his own dear self, and not without a cause. Do be kind, o Maharja, and allow your humble servant now to depart. He is helpless, for here he goes without good. And forgive, please, the sins and faults of this humble servant."

92 This statement is naturally made only in a relative sense, keeping in view the general information that we have about the unhappy economic situation of most of the artists. The buying power of the Rupee was considerable in those times and it is easy to see that on this amount a family could live in reasonable comfort in a village.

93 It is not unlikely that the holdings of the family were also added to after 1846 through purchase, etc., but the substantial part of

93 cont.
the land might well have come down as a hereditary property. The word ghumāon come probably from "as much land as can be ploughed by one pair of bullocks in a day" (Elliot's Supplemental Glossary, vol. II, p. 166). It later became a measure of land which varied in different parts of the country. In the Punjab the ghumāon generally consisted of 8 kanals.

94 Some signed or ascribed work by Harkhu and Chhajju is reproduced by Jagdish Mittal in "New Studies in Pahari Painting", Lalit Kala, no. 12. One can see that the work reflects the great style of the family from a previous generation, but is lacking in freshness and delicacy.

95 For a discussion of the jāgīr in Moghul India, see Irfan Habib, pp. 257-297. The word came originally perhaps from two Persian words, jāi gīr, literally meaning: "(one) holding or occupying a place". Wilson's Glossary (pp. 224-225) treats of the jāgīr in some detail and generally defines it as: "A tenure common under the Mohammadan government, in which the public revenues of a given tract of land were made over to a servant of the state, together with the powers requisite to enable him to collect and appropriate such revenue, and administer the general government of the district."

96 This comes very close to the idea of a khidmatī jāgīr or a muāfi. One can see that in the case of minor holders of these grants, claiming land revenue from others who cultivated the land must have been extremely difficult considering the number of references we find to the problems that arose between jāgīrdārs and cultivators over this. The painters are not likely to have tilled the land themselves, but those who did it for them, were really tenants taking a share of the produce and not paying land revenue to them.

97 This, as indicated before, applies to lands that were exempt from the payment of rent or tax etc. Persons holding muāfis were often called muāfīdārs, much as those who held jāgīrs were described as jāgīrdārs.

98 See above note no. 76. Wilson's Glossary, p. 13, defines it as: "Land granted by the Moghul Government,either rent-free or subject to a small quit-rent, to learned and religious persons of the Mohammedan faith, or for religious and charitable uses in relation to Mohammedanism. Such tenures were recognized by the British Government as hereditary and transferable".

99 This information comes from members of different families of artists in the hills. Sri Chandulal as much as Sri Gulabu Ram were explicit on this point.

1oo See table no. 17, Gazetteer of the Kangra District. It says that in 1868-69, skilled labour was paid at the rate of 5 Annas per day. From 1873-74 onwards, the highest rate for skilled labour was 8 Annas per day and the lowest 6 Annas.

1o1 This is a practice which continued throughout the British period in India, for it was a concise and fairly certain way of establishing the identity of a person. Here, the place of residence is only roughly given as Rihlu, because the taaluqa is identified rather than the specific village from which Gokal came.

1o2 See, thus, The Jakhbar Documents and The Pindori Documents. Among the instructions given to the officials and the functionaries, both of the state and of the jāgīrdārs, is that no resistance should be offered to the Mahants nor should they be asked to present new documents from year to year etc.

1o3 It was often, as Mr. V.S. Suri informed me, a matter of zor, literally "strength". It was perhaps much easier to obtain a grant on paper then to make it effective in fact!

1o4 See, for example, the document issued by Maharaja Sher Singh in S. 1898 to Sardar Lehna Singh Majithia which has as many as 1o official entries of endorsements etc. at its back. Indications that the contents had been noted or verified or examined or communicated all appear together with signatures and seals, among them those of Diwan Dina Nath and Narpat Rai.

1o5 "... the rapacity of the kardar was limited only by his discretion". The Gazetteer of the Kangra District, p. 219, describes the duties as also the general character of the kārdār in some detail. The duties were primarily fiscal, but also extended to matters of administration and law and order, making it possible for the kārdār to cast his net of corruption rather wide.

1o6 The chaudhuri, as Dr. Ifran Habib (p. 291-292) tells us, was "perhaps as important a functionary for the administration as the qanūngo; the qanūngo's work was largely directed toward the preparation of revenue assessment, the chaudhuri was chiefly concerned with its collection". For the chaudhuris, also see, The Jakhbar Documents, pp. 155-156; The Pindori Documents, pp. 116, note 13. Also see, Gazetteer of the Kangra District, 1883-84, p. 21o which mentions the police powers of the chaudhuris and the payments made to them.

1o7 These sketches come from practically every family of artists and large numbers of these have now entered museum collections such as those in the National Museum. For the most part, they consist of sketches or tinted drawings.

108 For begār or compulsory unpaid labour, see The Jakhbar Documents, p. 91, note 20; Irfan Habib, pp. 239, 240. The Gazetteer of the Kangra District, pp. 134-136, describes it as a custom "possessing the sanction of great antiquity in the hills". It indicates that some classes such as Brahmans and Rajputs were always exempt from it and the burden, "always a part of the burden of existence", fell principally upon agricultural classes.

109 This fits in also with the information that the wife of the painter would, at the end of the day, rub and massage his hands with ghee in order to make them retain their suppleness.

110 Sometimes the gap of time between the issue of one document and another exactly on the same subject is very slight. The clear in dication thus is that the repeated issue of documents on the same subject was not a function of time, but occasioned by different sets of circumstances. Both The Jakhbar Documents and The Pindori Documents provide instances in point.

111 The phrase muāf wa wāguzār ast which occurs frequently describes thus clearly an existing state and signifies that the thing is in-conferment already, free of rent. There is no suggestion in this construction that the grant is being restored.

112 Paintings of the Sikhs, pp. xvii-xviii.

113 These are collections of traditional episodes from the life of Guru Nank and have a place of great respect in the literature of the Sikh religion. A large number of Janam Sakhis were prepared, some embellished with paintings, and the Punjabi University at Patiala has a very considerable collection of these in documented form.

114 Chandigarh Museum nos. 2301-2377. The work may have been in the hand of Nikka or someone of that generation. The drawings are small in size, but extremely fluent.

115 See, Dosanj, S., and Uttam Singh, "A dated Janam Sakhi of Guru Nanak", Rooplekha, vol. XXXIX, no. 1.

116 The observation of Lt. Barr (Journal of a March from Delhi to Peshawur and from thence to Cabul, including travels in the Punjab. London 1844, pp. 69-71, 77-80, 81-83, 99-102) is remarkably sharp, if devoid of sympathy. He describes Krishna's exploits as painted on the gateway of the Royal Palace at Lahore in great detail, identifying separate scenes although generally commenting that "though no doubt considered in good taste by the Punjabees, to Englishmen they have a most ridiculous appearance." Of some murals at Gujranwala, he says that they were "by no means the most decorous in their description".

117 Virtually every _pandā_ at these temples is in possession of some _pattā_ or _parwānā_ recording a grant to some ancestor of his by Maharaja Ranjit Singh. The beautiful silver gates of the Kangra shrine were got prepared and installed by the Maharaja as humble offering.

118 I saw these entries through the courtesy of Sri Shashi Bhushan of Jwalamukhi whose assistance I wish thankfully to acknowledge here.

119 I saw a collection of these miniatures through the courtesy of Dr. Pritam Singh at Chandigarh.

12o See, Karuna Goswamy, "The frescoes of the Shish Mahal at Patiala", _Rooplekha_, vol. 38, nos. 1/2.

T h e T e x t

Transcriptions & Translations

ل

کاردار رہلو (مطلع) باشد

ماف عہ
نکا مصور را زمین کہ از قرار قدیم یکصد بیست وپنج روپیہ در
سالتمام مقرر
است بموجب سفارش سردار بدہ سنگہ جی عطا شدہ بود
باید کہ بدستور سابق بہ مشار الیہ واگذار سازند کار بیگار معاف شدہ
اندرینباب تاکید مزید دانند
تحریر ۳۱ ماہ اسوج ۱۸۸۲ سمہ پروانگے حضور ڈیرہ رام باغ

زبانے راجہ صاحب جیو

I

O(nkār)[1]

(Seal)[2]
May the Immortal (God)
be the Protector

The personal seal

(Seal)[3]
May the Immortal (God)
be the Protector

Ranjit Singh

May the kārdār of Rihlu be hereby informed:[4]

The painter Nikka has been, from olden times,[5] in possession of land valued at rupees one hundred and twenty five (Rs. 125/-) per annum. This grant of land has been confirmed upon him at the recommendation of Sardar Budh Singh Ji.[6] It is ordered that the land should be left with him and without his being subject to render any (usual) service[7] or begār.[8] In this matter this should be treated as a strict injunction.

Written on the 31st of the month of Asūj, S. 1882. Under orders of the Huzūr[9] at Camp: Rambagh.[10]

(In the margin)

(Conveyed) verbally through Raja Sahib Jio.[11]

ا

او جلدیدار گنڈا مل کاردار رہلو مسرور باشند

آنچه زمین سرکار والا در وجه نکا مصور از حضور والا
بخشیده شد پوره آدای کرده بدهند درین باب
توقف نگردد حسب المسطور بعمل آرند. تحریر بتاریخ ۲۳ ماگھ
سنه ۱۸۸۲ پروانگی راجه صاحب زبانی میاں کیسری سنگه تحریر یافت

این بار همراه ایضاً صحت شد ذمه ایشان است
و هرچه نذرانه از مشار الیه ادائی باشد درینجائی نگیرند
در خانه مشار الیه اصلاً تعدی نرسانند
بموجب پروانه سرکار زمین پوره کرده بدهند

II

O(nkār)[1]

(In Tākri)[2]

" Sahi "[3]

May the Pure of Countenance,[4] Ganda Mal, Kardar of Rihlu, remain in peace and happiness:

Now, the land belonging to the noble Sarkar[5] which has been granted to the painter Nikka by the exalted Huzūr should be given to him in full measure.[6] In this matter there should be no delay and you should act in accordance with (instructions contained in these) lines.

Written on the 23rd of the month of Magh, S. 1882.

This has been written under the orders of Raja Sahib as conveyed verbally through Mian Kesri Singh.[7]

(In the margin)

This time it is your responsibility that there should be no error. Whatever nazrana[8] may be payable by the aforesaid (Nikka), it should not be withheld there. You should (also) not cause any hardship to the household of the aforesaid (Nikka).[9] The entire land according to the parwana of the Sarkar should be handed over.

نقل پٹہ سری راجہ رنجیت سنگھ

سنہ عیسوی ...
نواب گورنر جنرل
بہادر
صاحب

عاملان حال و استقبال تعلقہ ہری پور و گلیر مسرور باشند
درینوقت جاگیر بمقابلہ یکصد روپیہ سالتمام ابتداء فصل ربیع سنہ ۱۸۹۴
در طلب و نوکری دروجہ گوکل مصور از تعلقہ گلیر واقعہ
موضع رام گرھ عطا و مرحمت گردید باید کہ ابتدای موصوف جاگیر دروجہ معز الیہ
از تعلقہ آنمسطور واگذار داشتہ احدی مزاحم نبودہ باشد دستخط او جلد دیدار سردار لہنا سنگھ
سندھانوالہ حاضر نمایند و در حساب مجرا شناسند و ... غایت باشد

بتاریخ ۹ ماہ ماگھ سنہ ۱۸۹۳

پروانگی حضور

۱۱ جون ۱۸۴۶ء کو نقل پٹہ ہذا دی گئی

III

O(nkār)

Copy of the pattā of Shri Raja Ranjit Singh[1]

(In the margin)
"Rs. 14 and 11 annas."

Illegible

Signatures in English

(Seal)[3]

"... Sahib Bahadur,
Nawab Governor General
A.D. ....."

May the present and the future āmils[4] of the taaluqa of Haripur and Guler remain in peace and happiness:

Now, a jagir[5] valued for rupees one hundred (the half of which is fifty) per annum, beginning from the Rabi'[6] crop of Samvat 1894, has been conferred with great kindness upon the painter Gokal, in the mauza of Ramgarh[7] in the taaluqa of Guler, as retainer and pay for his services.[8] It is ordered that with effect from the aforesaid date the jagir granted to this worthy person should be handed over to him. No one should offer any obstruction in this matter. The signatures of that person of Pure Countenance, Sardar Lehna Singh Sandhanwalia, should be obtained (by way of attestation) and sent here.[9] The jagir should be included in the State Accounts and every kindness should be shown to its incumbent.[10]

Dated the 9th of the month of Magh, S. 1893.

(In the margin)
Issued under the orders of the Exalted one.

(On the reverse)
A copy of this patta was issued on June 11, 1846.[11]

پروانه

اوجل دیدار کاهنه سنگه کنگ مسرور باشند

باید که بورود پروانه بموجب پروانه سرکار والا
جاگیر دروجه گوکل مصور ملازم سردار صاحب
عطر سنگه واگذار کرده دهند و بموجب پروانه عالے
عمل نمایند زمین عمده لاهرط ... دریںباب تاکید مزید انگاشته
حسب المسطور بعمل آرند تحریر بتاریخ ۲۳ ماه ساون ۱۸۹۴ سمه

پروانگی حضور ڈیره لاهور

نقل کتابت کرده شد

IV

A(kāl) P(urkh)[1]

"Authenticated"[2]

May the Pure of Countenance, Kahan Singh Kang,[3] remain in peace and happines:

It is ordered that upon receipt of this parwāna, which is issued in accordance with the parwāna of the exalted Sarkar,[4] the jāgir in respect of the painter Gokal, employee of Sardar Sahib Attar Singh,[5] should be handed over to him. The exalted parwāna should be acted upon and lāhar[6] land of good quality should be given to him. Recognizing this to be a strict injunction, you should act in accordance with (the instructions contained in) these lines.[7]

Written on the 25th of the month of Sawan S. 1894.[8]

Under the orders of the Huzur[9] at Camp Lahore.

(On the reverse)

"Duly copied."[10]

ل.

ارادت نشان لاله کاهنه سنگه مسرور باشند

بعد از توجهات فراوان واضح باد چون زمین
جاگیر دروجه گوکل مصور ملازم خالصه جیو از حضور خاقانے
معاف وواگذاراست حالا مشارالیه را پروانه واگذاری زمین
از راجه صاحب جیو نولیسانیده داده معز الیه بمعه پروانه خالصه جیو
و پروانه راجه صاحب جیو مردان خیر خواه میباشد لازم که
زمین عمده لایق زراعت دروجه گوکل مصور خواهد داد
معز الیه معامله آنجا میگرفته باشد اصلاً درینمقدمه فرق نسازند
که مشارالیه ملازم خالصه جیواست تاکید مزید شناسند
الطاف والا متوجه الحال خود شناسند تحریر بتاریخ ۲۵ ساون

V

A(kāl) P(urkh)

(Seal)[1]
May the Immortal (God)
be the Protector

Ajit Singh
1893

May the well-intentioned Lala Kahan Singh[2] remain in peace and happiness:

After profuse expressions of (our) kindness,[3] it is clearly stated that jāgīr land, free of rent, is in conferment by the exalted Huzūr upon the painter, Gokal, employee of the Khalsa Jio.[4] Now, a parwāna regarding the grant of this land has been got written by the Raja Sahib Jio and given to him.[5] This worthy man who has the parwāna of the Khalsa Jio and that of the Raja Sahib Jio is among the devoted servants[6] (of the Court). It is imperative that good, culturable land[7] should be given to the painter Gokal, so that he becomes entitled to receive the revenues from it. In this matter no deviation (from these orders) at all should be made, for the aforementioned (Gokal) is an employee of the Khalsa Jio. Know this to be a strict injunction, and expect every kindness for yourself.[8]

Written on the 25th of Sawan.[9]

(Reverse: In Takri)[1o]

(Patta of) Sardar Jit Singh Sandhanwalia[11] regarding the jagir in Guler.

بفضل سری اکال پورکهہ جیو

برہمورت مصر میا داس مسرور شود

بعد توجہات فراواں مطالعہ نمایند آنکہ جاگیر مسمی گوکل مصور
در تعلقہ رام گڈھ واقع است و ظاہر آدمان (؟) ... خلش
و خجالت بیجا از تنبول و بہاڑے و غیرہ می رسانند
لہذا نگارش می رود کہ از جاگیر مصور مذکور کدام ہیچ
خلش و خجالت بیجا نرسانند تاکید دانستہ حسب المرقوم

بعمل آرند

قدغن شدید شناسند مرقوم ۲۵ اسوج ۱۸۹۷ سمہ

پروانگے حضور زبانے میاں میراں بخش. توقف در نگ

By the Grace of the Immortal Being[1]

"Shri Ram Ji"[2]

(Seal)[3]
May the Immortal (God)
be the Protector

Ajit Singh

May the image of Brahma,[4] Missar Mayya Das,[5] remain in peace and happiness:

After expression of profuse kindness, you are informed that, with regard to the *jagir* of the painter Gokal situated in the *taaluqa* of Ramgarh, it has been reported that some persons ... are causing unnecessary trouble and harassment (to the painter) in respect of *tambul*[7] and *bhati* etc. It is accordingly being written that in regard to the *jagir* of the aforesaid painter, no trouble or harassment should be caused. Knowing this to be an injunction,[8] (you) should act strictly in accordance with the (instructions contained in this) writing. Know this matter to be worthy of strict care.

Written on the 25th of Asuj, S. 1897.[9]

Under orders of the *Huzur* as verbally conveyed by Mian Miran Bakhsh during the halt at Drang.[10]

ل

سری واہگورو جیکے پیارے ست گورو جیکے سنوارے مشفق مہربان مصدر تلطفات بیکران

بھائی صاحب سردار لہنا سنگھ جیو سلمہ.

بعد فتح واہگورو جیکے و شوق ملاقات فرحت آیات کہ خلاصہ مطالبات باطنی است منکشف بضمیر برضا نظیر باد در ینجاے بفضل ستگورو جیو عافیت است و صحت تندرستے مزاج مبارک از درگاہ سری مہاراج جیو شب و روز مطلوب مخلصی نوازد (؟) آنکہ تہمت خون بذمہ چھجو چتیرہ بموجب دعوی اہل عرضان کارپردازان سری کانگڑہ جیو نمودہ بود چون برہمن از انجا آمدہ بود و خالصہ جیو بقسم و سوگند از برہمن مسطور استفسار نمودہ و موسی الیہ

تمام سرگذشت بیان نمود/ واز اظہارش چنان بوضوح پیوستہ کہ مشار الیہ را ناحق/ متہم ساختہ اندبرای ہمین باز بخدمت سامے متصدعہ شدہ دستور عنوان (؟)/ و گورسہاے جمعدار مامور ساختہ تولاکہ توجہات کریمانہ بحال ہرکہو چتیرہ کہ از ملازمان خالصہ جیو است مبذول فرمودہ مخلصے/ ورستنگارش (؟) سازند زیادہ تحریر چہ نگارد

VII

O(nkar)[1]

May[2] the beloved of the Sacred Guru, the recipient of the favours of the True One, kind and beneficent, the object of Infinite Bounties, dear Brother, Sardar Lehna Singh Jio,[3] remain under Divine Protection:[4]

After the greeting, "Victory be to the Guru," and the expression of my fervent desire which is the essence of innermost wishes,.... I wish to say that with the True Guru's grace all here is well and I pray for your health and good cheer, day and night, at the altar of the Merciful and Divine Lord.

(The purpose of writing this missive is) that the painter Chhajju has been charged with murder[5] (in a case instituted by the complainants) before the officials of Shri Kangra Jio.[6] Now, a Brahmin from that place (Kangra) has come here and I have questioned him already, making him swear sacred oaths about this whole business. He has narrated to me the entire incident and from his testimony it is evident that the said person (the painter, Chhajju) has been falsely implicated. For this reason he has been directed to approach you; the Jamadar Gur Sahai being deputed for this purpose.[7] It is desired that keeping in view that the painter Harkhu, who is in my service, is deserving of our favours,[8] this man (Chhajju, his brother) should be exonerated and released.

What else is there to say?[9]

۱

بفضل سری اکال پورکهه جیو

او جلدیدار نرمل بدهسنگه سردار باوقار سردار لهنا سنگه مجیتهیه مسرور باشند

آنکه جاگیر مبلغ دوصد وبیست وپنج روپیه ماد عے سال تمام بموجب تفصیل ذیل
دروجه گوکل مصور که سابق نزد سرداران سندهانواله ملازم بود
مقرراست باید که بدستور سابق درنوکری از ابتدائی فصلخریف سنه ۱۸۹۸
واگذارند که مشارالیه درحضور انور حاضر و ملازم شده

ماد عے له

از تعلقه رهلو	از تعلقه هری پور
ماد عے	مار

بموجب آئین دفتر معلی مطلع شد
و مهر ونشانی
تحریر بتاریخ ۱۸ ماه مگهر سنه ۱۸۹۸ پروانگی حضور ڈیره سری امرتسر جیو
رام باغ ...

O(nkār)

By the grace of the Immortal being

Sd/- (In French)

"Cher Singh"[1]

(Sher Singh)

(Seals)[2]

A. May the Immortal (God) be the Protector

Sher....[3]

B. May the Immortal (God) be the Protector

"Inscribed"

C. May the Immortal (God) be the Protector

"The writer of Pattas"[4]

1887

May the Pure of Countenance, Subtle of Intellect, the Sardar of Glory, Sardar Lehna Singh Majithia, remain in peace and happiness:[5]

Whereas, jāgīr valued at rupees two hundred and twenty five (Rs. 225, the half of which is rupees 112, annas eight) per annum, as per details[6] given below, is in conferment upon the painter Gokal who was formerly in the employment of the Sandhanwalia Sardars.[7] It is ordered that this (jāgīr) should remain with him as of old in lieu of his service, since the aforesaid (Gokal) has now presented himself before the illustrious Huzūr and has been employed.[8]

(Detail) : Rs. 225/-

In the taaluqa of Rihlu	In the taaluqa of Haripur
Rs. 125/-	Rs. 1oo/-

(In the margin)

Noted in the Dafter-i-Mu'alla[8] as per the regulations and the seal and marks (on this parwana).

Written on the 18th of the month of Maghar, 1898. Under orders of the Huzūr at Camp Ram Bagh in Shri Amritsar Jio.

(On the reverse)[9]

1. "Noted".
2. "Inscribed".
3. "Examined".
4. Seal: "May the Immortal (God) be the Protector". Narpat Rai.
5. "Verified".
6. "18th of the month of Maghar: Dewan Dina Nath"[1o]
7. No. ... of patta of the Daftar-i-Dewani
8. (Illegible)
9. "Entered".

او

اکال سہائے
باوا لچھمن سنگھ

ارادت نشان چودھری چوہڑ مسرور باشند

چوں جاگیر بمقابلہ مبلغ دوصد بیست و پنج روپیہ ~~عہ~~ از سرکار والا
در وجہ گوکل مصور ابتدای خریف سنہ ۹۸ معاف گردیدہ
باید کہ جاگیر مفصلہ ذیل بموجب پروانہ سرکار والا

تعلقہ رہلو	تعلقہ ہری پور
عہ	~~ر~~

بدہند واگذار دارند دریں باب تاکید است
تحریر بتاریخ ۲۷ ماہ مگھر سنہ ۱۸۹۸

IX

O(nkār)

(Seal)[1]
May the Immortal (God)
be the Protector

Bawa Lachhman Singh.

May the well-intentioned Chaudhari[2] Chuhar remain in peace and happiness![3]

Whereas, a jāgir of the value of rupees two hundred and twenty five (Rs. 225/-) (per annum) has been conferred as a muāfi[4] upon the painter Gokal with effect from the Kharif (crop) of S. 98.[5] It is ordered that the jāgīr as detailed below and in accordance with the parwāna of the exalted Sarkar,[6] should be handed over to him.

In the taaluqa of Rihlu	In the taaluqa of Haripur
Rs. 125/-	Rs. 1oo/-

On this behalf this is an injunction.
Written on the 27th of the month of Maghar, S. 1898.[7]

اکال سہائے

باوا لچھمن سنگھ خصوصیت و موالات نشان مہربان دوستان بھگت بھگوشاه
مسرور باشند

۹ا عـ
درینولا جاگیر بمقابله مبلغ دوصد بیست و پنج روپیه در وجه گوکل
مصور مفصله ذیل بموجب پروانه سرکار والا ابتدای فصل خریف ۹۸ سنه

در تعلقه ربلو	هری پور
ما عـ	مار

واگذار گردیده باید که مطابق پروانه والا جاگیر مشار الیه
واگذار کرده دهند توقف نسازند درینباب تاکید است
تحریر بتاریخ ۲۷ ماه مگهر سنه ۱۸۹۸

و پروانه نزد خود دارند
که شائے الحال سند گردد تاکید است
بیض

O(nkār)

(Seal)[1]
May the Immortal (God)
be the Protector

Bawa Lachhman Singh

May the distinguished and well-intentioned, the benefactor of friends, Bhagat Boghu Shah[2] remain in peace and happiness:

Now, a jāgīr valued at rupees two hundred and twenty five (Rs. 225) (per annum) is in conferment upon the painter Gokal beginning from the Kharif crop of S. 1898 according to the parwana of the exalted Sarkar as per the following details:

In the taaluqa of Rihlu	In the taaluqa of Haripur
Rs. 125/-	Rs. 1oo/-

It is ordered that, in accordance with the exalted parwāna, the jāgīr[4] of the aforesaid (Gokal) should be handed over to him. There should be no delay in the matter. This is an injunction in this matter.[5]

Written on the 27th of the month of Maghar, S. 1898.[6]

(In the margin)

This parwana should be kept by him so that it serves as a sanad for the future.[7] This is an injunction. Baiz.[8]

اکال سہائے
لہنا سنگھ

ارادت نشان بہگت بوہگو شاہ مسرور باشند

سابق ازین مبلغ دوصد روپیہ سالتمام دروجہ فوجو مصور ملازم راجہ صاحب سرگباشے

بقرار قدیم مقرر بود حالا دروجہ ہرکہو مصور عوض آن عطاے شدہ

پروانہ حضور والا درباب دادن مبلغ صادر گردیدہ ازینموجب ارشاد حضور

بنام شما صادر شدہ لازم کہ جاگیر مبلغات مذکور بمشارالیہ واگذارند رسید

وپروانہ سرکار بگیرند

قدغن باشند تحریر بتاریخ ۲۰ اسوج سمہ ۹۹ پروانگے حضور ڈیرہ لاہور

بتاریخ

قلمبند ۲۰ اسوج

سمہ ۹۹

درج کتاب

XI

In Gurmukhi[1]
"as per the Parwana"

(Seal)[2]
May the Immortal (God)
be the Protector,

Lehna Singh

May the well intentioned Bhagat Bohgu Shah[3] remain in peace and happiness:

Formerly, (land valued at)[4] rupees two hundred per annum had been in conferment upon the painter Fauju,[5] employee of the late Raja Sahib,[6] in accordance with the established practice of old. Now this (land) has been granted to the painter Harkhu in his place, and a parwāna regarding the payment of this amount (to Harkhu) has been issued by the exalted Huzur.[7] Accordingly, this order of the Exalted One has been issued in your name. It should be seen to that the jāgīr of the value of the aforesaid amount should be handed over to the abovementioned (Harkhu) and a receipt of the same as also of the parwāna should be obtained.

In this matter every care should be taken.[8]

Written on the 2oth of Asuj, S. 1899 under personal orders of the Huzūr (at) Camp : Lahore.

On the reverse:
"Entered in the Register."
"Inscribed on the 2oth of Asuj, (V.S.) 1899."

پچھجو مصور بداند

[illegible]

باید که آنکه مبلغ دو صد و بیست و پنج روپیه
زمین بایشان واگذار است فرماید که
بورود پروانه والا از زمین مذکور نصفا نصف همراه گوکل مصور
کرده بگیرند و آنکه زمین عمده است نصف از آن
عمده و نصفی از زمین دیگر تقسیم کرده بدهند
تاکید شناسند باز عرض مشار الیه در حضور نرسد

و آنکه غله ایمه است آنهم نصفا نصفی
کرده حواله گوکل سازند تاکید است

O(nkār)

"Glory to Shri Rama"[1]

Be it known to the painter Chhajju:[2]

That land valued at rupees two hundred and twenty five (Rs. 225/-) (the half of which is Rs. one hundred and twelve, annas eight only), is under their (family) occupation.[3] It is hereby ordered that, upon receipt of this exalted parwāna,[4] this land should be shared half and half with the painter Gokal.[5] The division should be made in such a way that he (Gokal) should be given half of whatever land there is of good quality, and half of the other type.[6] This should be treated as an injunction, (so that) no further representation is received (has to be made by) the abovementioned person (Gokal).

(In the margin)

Further, the produce from this ai'mma (land)[7] should also be divided half and half and (his share) handed over to Gokal. This is a strict order.[8]

عزیز از جان لاله سوهنا مل جی

بموجب فرموده آنصاحب باطیه چھجو مصور

فرستاده امید که پروانه و تنخواه بنام توشخانه

نویسانیده دهند که قرار شکرگذار بوده باشد

الراقم بنده درگاه ناراین چودهری

XIII

Dearer than Life, Lala Sohna Mal Ji:[1]

In accordance with the orders of the <u>Sahib</u>,[2] the amount sanctioned for the painter Chhajju may be got despatched. A <u>parwana</u> pertaining to his salary,[3] and addressed to the <u>toshakhaha</u>,[4] may be issued; This will give (me) cause for much gratitude.

Written by the humble servant of the Court,[5] Narayan Chaudhry.

متصدیان دفتر معلے

ابتدای ۸ ماه جیٹھ سنہ ۱۹۰۰ گوکل مصور ولد نیکا ابن نین سوکھہ ساکن رہلو

تفصیل

رسد	سی سری ماه	زمین جاگیر (؟)
۶۰۶٫	عـصـم	

نوکرداشته شد باید که از اقرار صحیح خاص اسم مشار الیه درج دفتر سازند

۱۰ ماه جیٹھه سنه ۱۹۰۰

XIV

(In Tākri)

"Shri Ram Ji."[1]

"The jagir of Gokal Ram"

(To the) Mutasaddis[2] of the Daftar-i-Mu'alla[3] (Exalted Office).

Beginning from the 8th of the month of Jeth, of (V.S.) 19oo, the painter Gokal son of Nikka, son of Nainsukh, resident of taaluqa Rihlu,[4] has been entered as an employee[5] (on the following terms).

(Detail)

Rations[6]	Every month[7]	Land Jagir[8](?)
6 1/2 seers	3o (?)	

It is ordered that the name of the aforesaid (Gokal) should, in accordance with the special authentication to this effect, be entered in the records.[9]

(In the margin)

Dated the 1oth of the month of Jeth, S. 19oo.

(On the reverse)

"Examined." (Carried out?)[1o]

بفضل سری اکال پورکهه جیو

او جلدیدار وزیر کرم سنگه مسرور باشند

اکال سهائے
رنجودسنگه

آنکه مبلغ یکصد روپیه سالتمام را اراضی از تعلقه هری پور درو جه
(نصف)
گوکل مصور از حضور انور معاف است باید که بدستور سابق
از ابتدای فصل خریف ۱۹۰۲ سمه واگذار دارند که پروانه معافی انوری
از سر نو بنام خالصه جیو صادر است بموجب صحیح خاص و مهر و نشانے
بشمار هجری است تحریر بتاریخ ۱۶ مانگهه سمه ۱۹۰۳

ڈیره گذرتلون
سابق واگذار است دروجه چهجو مصور
از تعلقه رهلو
سالتمام
دروجه مشارالیه

XV

By the Grace of the Immortal being

(In Gurmukhi)[1]
The amount of Rs. One hundred
according to the parwana.
Rs. 1oo/-

(Seal)[2]
"May the Immortal (God)
be the Protector."

Ranjodh Singh.

May the Pure of Countenance, Wazir Karam Singh,[3] remain in peace and happiness:

Now, land valued at rupees one hundred (the half of which is Rs. 5o/-)[4] is in conferment as a muafi by the resplendent Sarkar, upon the painter Gokal. It is ordered that this should continue to be so, as before, from the beginning of the Kharif crop of (Samvat) 19o2. A parwana of muafi from the exalted Sarkar has been issued in this regard once again to the Khalsa Jio,[5] complete with personal authentication[6] and seal and signs. This should be entered into your accounts.

Written on the 16th of Magh (V.S.) 19o2.

At the Talwan Crossing.[7]

(Detail)[8]

Rs. 15o/-

Already in conferment upon the painter Chhajju in the taaluqa of Rihlu: Rs. 5o per annum

(In conferment upon) the aforesaid (Gokal): Rs. 1oo-oo.

(On the reverse)

In Takri : Samvat 19o2, Magh pravishte 16.

Sat Sri Akal

Inscribed,
Written on the 16th of the month of Magh, 19o2.
Entered in the Register on 17th of Magh, 19o2.

سید ہادی
حسین خاں

۸ جولائی ۱۸۴۶ء

مبلغ مدعے بابت معاملہ اراضی ... گھمانو ازان
دا ئودر مصور واقع رجولے کے بتحویل تاراچند تحویلدار بصیغہ
امانت داخل خزانہ محال ہوے اسواسطے یہ رسید
لکھ دی کہ سند ہووے فقط

العبد

کالکا دیال سیاہہ نویس

XVI

(Seal)[1]
Sayyad Hadi
Hussain Khan.

8th of July, A.D. 1846.[2]

The amount of Rs. 13 has been paid into the treasury of the *mahal*[3] as trust, on account of land revenue due on land measuring ...*ghumaons*[4] from the painter Damodar of Rajoli through Tara Chand Tahwildar.[5] This receipt has been issued as a *sanad* for this purpose.[6]

Faqat.(This is all)

(In the margin)
"The slave[7] (that is, the mark of the signatures of)
Kalka Dayal, *Siyahanawis*"[8]

In Takri)
"Rs. 13....".

سید ہادی

حسین خاں

۱۰ ستمبر سنہ ۱۸۴۶ء

مبلغ عـــ ۰۶ر بابت اراضی للعـــ گہما نو مضبوطہ واقع موضع رجوے تعلقہ ریلو
ازاں دامودر مصور معاملہ ربیع سنہ ۱۹۰۳ معرفت دامودر مذکور بتحویل
تاراچند تحویلدار امانت خزانہ محال ہوا اسواسطہ یہ رسید دی گئی۔

عـــ
۰۶ر

سود	اصل
۰۶ر	عـــ

XVII

(Seal)
Sayyad
Hadi Hussain Khan

1oth of September, (A.D.) 1846.[1]

The amount of rupees 15, 6 annas and 6 pies has been received from the painter Damodar on account of revenue due for the Rabi crop of S. 19o3[2] on 14 ghumaons of land now 'confiscated'[3] in the mauza[4] of Rajoli[5] in the taaluqa of Rihlu, through Tara Chand Tahwildar. This amount has been deposited in the treasury of the mahal in trust. This receipt is therefore issued (for the said amount).

(Detail)

Rs. 15, annas 6, pies 6.

Principal	Interest[6] (?)
Rs. 15/-	6 annas and 6 pies.

(In the margin)

In Takri, an entry which begins with the words:
"Rs. 15, 6 annas and 6 pies....."

یکم ماہ نومبر سنہ ۱۸۴۶ء

داخلہ ۱۰ للعہ روپیہ بابت معاملہ فصل خریف سنہ ۱۹۰۳ قسط ماہ نومبر از دامودر مصور ۲ بابت زر اراضے معافی کہ ضبط ہوئی واقع رجو لے تعلقہ رہلو معرفت تاراچند تحویلدار داخل خزانہ سرکار ہوے اسواسطہ (رسید) دیاگیا

سرک	نقد
۲	۱۰ للعہ
	۱۰

بحساب سرکار در معاملہ خریف تحریر شد

XVIII

Receipt[1]

First of the month of November, A.D. 1846.

Received rupees forty two and two annas, on account of the instalment[2] of land revenue for the Kharif crop,[3] due in the month of November, V.S. 19o3, on the confiscated muafi[4] (land) in mauza Rajoli in the taaluqa of Rihlu from the painter Damodar through Tara Chand Tahwildar. This amount has been paid into the State Treasury and is, therefore, acknowledged.

(Seal)
..... Din

(Detail)

Principal	Interest[5] (?)
Rs. 41, 1o annas and 6 pies.	7 annas and 6 pies.

Entered in the State account of revenue for the Kharif crop.

(In margin)
In Takri: "Rs. 42, two annas....."

منشی هادی

حسین خاں

۲۷ جنوری ۱۸۴۷ء

مدخله مبلغ ــــلل روپیه بابت معامله فصلخریف ۱۹۰۳ سنه
قسط ماه جنوری ۱۸۴۷ء از موضع رجولے رابار اضے که مضبطه
دامودر مصور معرفت تاراچند تحویلوار
داخل خزانه سرکار هوے اسواسطه داخل رسانند (؟)

اصل	سود (؟)
عـلل	۶ر
۱۱ر	۶ پائی

بحساب سرکار در معامله خریف محرر شد

XIX

(Seal)[1]
Munshi Hadi
Hussain Khan

Receipt

27th of January, 1847.

Received rupees forty three, one anna and 6 pies, on account of instalment[2] of land revenue for the *Kharif* crop, due in the month of January, 1847 as the confiscated *(jagir)* land in *mauza* Rajoli in possession of the painter, Damodar, through Tara Chand Tahwildar. The amount has been paid into the State Treasury and is, therefore, acknowledged.[3]

(Detail)[4]

Principal	Interest
Rs. 42,	6 annas and
11 annas	6 pies.

Entered in the State account of revenue of the *Kharif* crop.

XX

(In Hindi)[1]

May the Noble Maharani[2] remain always in peace and safety:

Respectful greetings of "Victory to the Lord"[3] at your feet from the humble slave,[4] the painter Saudagar. Now, the exalted order issued by you through the official, Shankar Datt, has reached this slave. It is in that connection that I present this humble petition with hope... In the days of the late Maharaja,[5] a cash salary of rupees fifteen per mensem and supplies of rations were given[6] (to this servant). But, in addition, generous rewards were lavished (by the Maharaja).[7] Now, my family is hard put to it to survive on these fifteen rupees.[8] For this reason, I beg that my case should be reconsidered and a fresh order (regarding my remuneration) be kindly issued.

I have written humbly what I thought was proper.

(Amendments in the text)[9]

"(I) used to be sustained through many other favours also of which you are undoubtedly aware. This slave's father.....

Further, you are wiser and older than us and we all feed at your kindness. All our lives we are devoted to you. We should be so taken care of that we should be under eternal gratitude to you and our families and children should pray for you, out of gratefulness. As for the rest, you are our master and we are in all circumstances your slaves."

NOTES TO I

1 The alif here stands fairly clearly for Omkār which serves as the auspicious sar-i-nāmah much like the Allāh-u-Akbar in Muslim documents. In some cases alif is followed by a wau to make omkār more explicit as in The Pindori Documents, nos. 2o, 22, 28, etc. At the same time only alif appears in many documents such as nos. 22, 23, 26, etc.

2 The formula Akal Sahai used in the seal is only too well-known to us from other Sikh documents (see The Pindori Documents for numerous examples). This seal bears also the words muhr-i-khās signifying the personal seal of the Maharaja. This corresponds closely to the auzak on the Mughal documents.

3 This is apparently the same seal that appears in no. XXXV of The Pindori Documents. The appearance of this seal together with the other one indicates that while the personal seal might have been carried on the person of the Maharaja or a very close and high official, the seal bearing his name must have been in the charge of an official empowered to fix it on documents issued on behalf of the Maharaja.

4 This rather summary way of addressing an official is in contrast to the more elaborate or personal way suggested by the formula in other documents saying that the addressee "may remain in peace and happiness".

5 This is a reference, in all probability, to grants in favour of Nikka by some Rajput Chief like Raj Singh of Chamba or Sansar Chand of Kangra. Such a grant might have formed the basis for a request by Nikka that his "jāgīr" be allowed to remain in conferment upon him.

6 Even though Budh Singh is not fully identified here, there is no doubt, considering the group of document as a whole, that it is Budh Singh Sandhanwalia who is meant. The recommendation by Budh Singh on behalf of Nikka is of interest and significance as pointed out in the introduction.

7 The exact connotation of kār is not clear here. While it is possible that it is only an insignificant adjunct to begār which follows, it is not unlikely that it has a precise connotation such as work which was compulsory like begār but which was, unlike begār, paid for.

8 The exemption from forced, unpaid labour must have been important for the painters and it would have been necessary for them to quote authority while claiming exemption from it, when a local official demanded it. It is an important concession and was frequently introduced in documents of this kind. See, thus, The Documents of

8 cont.
Jahangir in The Jakhbar Documents, pp. 76-1o1. The Gazetteer of the Kangra District, pp. 134-136, draws attention to these "deeds of immunity" being issued in favour of individuals.

9 This refers clearly to the Maharaja and is one of the few words which, as becomes clear from documents such as these, were exclusively used to indicate the ruler.

1o This is, in all likelihood, Rambagh in Amritsar which was frequently visited by the Maharaja while in that city.

11 Even though there were many people bearing the title Raja at the Lahore court, Raja Sahib Jio was used apparently only for Raja Dhyan Singh, the great Dogra Chief who was extremely close to the Maharaja and was his principal advisor.

1 It is significant that this document does not bear a seal. There is clear mention here that it has been drawn up at the asking of Raja Dhyan Singh, but no seal appears, possibly because the Raja did not use one at all.

2 Takri is the notoriously illegible script of the hills which seems to have endless varieties of its own. While formal documents in the hills often used Persian, as in the plains, personal correspondence or documents almost always employed Takri. The large number of inscriptions tht we find on Pahari Paintings are in this script, sometimes in its most unnegotiable form. It is interesting that the mark of approval, sahī is in Takri here in place of Gurmukhi which one would normally expect in Sikh documents. This comes apparently from the fact that Raja Dhyan Singh was a Rajput himself, coming from Jammu.

3 This is in token of the issuing authority confirming that the document has been drawn up as per orders correctly. The letter sād often appears on Muslim documents and can be interpreted both as sādiq and sahīh, both words meaning "correct". See, thus, The Jakhbar Documents, no. IX; The Pindori Documents, nos. XI, XII. This form of the word is obviously a corruption of Persian sahīh.

4 The words ujjal didār seem to have been frequently employed as honorifics at the Sikh court. See, thus, no. XL of The Pindori Documents as also some other documents in this collection.

5 This is probably a reference to khālisa lands even though theoretically all land would perhaps be referred to as "belonging to the noble sarkār".

6 There is suggestion here, which is supported by the emphatic note in the margin, that the land was not given to Nikka in full measure by the kārdār or some other local functionary following the original orders of the Maharaja (Document I) of nearly four months earlier. Apparently Nikka complained about this matter and this emphatic instruction is then issued.

7 Mian Kesri Singh is probably the same as Rai Kesri Singh who was very close to the Jammu Rajas and finds frequent mention in the records of the times. He was especially close to Raja Suchet Singh. He was killed along with Suchet Singh in March 1844 and three widows of his committed sati at Samba in the Jammu hills.

8 This suggests that while several imposts were not levied on a grantee like Nikka here, customary gifts such as this nazrāna spoken of here continued to be offered by the grantee. It is interesting

8 cont.

to see that Raja Dhyan Singh instructs the kārdār to forward the nazrāna, perhaps to Lahore, and not to keep it there.

9 The polite address at the beginning notwithstanding, the tone of this document is firm and almost one of annoyance at the previous (mis)conduct of the kardar. The "hardship" being caused to the household of Nikka finds unusual mention here: perhaps Nikka was having truly difficult times with this official.

NOTES TO III

1 This is a note right at the top introduced to indicate that the document that follows is not the original but a copy. The note must have been placed at the time that the copy was made and not later. Notice the respectful way in which Ranjit Singh is described. This is different than the seals which use no honorifics after the invocation of the deity.

2 It is not clear what this amount signifies. As suggested in the introduction, however, this may be a rough calculation of the amount of revenue to be imposed on this land once the decision had been taken by the British authorities to resume jāgīrs such as these and give them back to their owners on new terms which included payment of land rent.

3 It has unfortunately not been possible either to read the signatures or to decipher the seal fully. There is no doubt, however, that this seal was placed for authenticating this copy of the original document issued by Maharaja Ranjit Singh.

4 The āmil was an official in the pargana entrusted with the twin duty of assessing and collecting the revenue. Wilson's Glossary indicates that the position of the āmils changed in later times, for the āmil is defined therein not only as an "officer of Government in the financial department, especially a collector of revenue on the part of the Government", but also as "the farmer of the revenue". See The Jakhbar Documents, p. 68, note 12, and The Pindori Documents, p. 97, note 6.

5 This is the first time that the word jāgīr appears in these documents. As noted, however, this jāgīr is probably to be understood only as a land grant free of rent.

6 This is the spring-harvest, the autumn harvest being referred to as kharīf. It is interesting that these Persian names are retained for the crops in the Sikh documents.

7 This makes it a fresh grant, different from the grant worth Rupees 125 given to Nikka, father of Gokal, which is referred to in Documents I and II. If this construction is not placed, then one has to conclude that the original grant was reduced, something that is a little unlikely if Gokal's family continued to be in favour.

8 It is difficult to exactly translate the talab-wa-naukri of the original. The suggestion is that this grant is in payment of services with the further implication that Gokal could be required to be present whenever wanted.

9 As pointed out in the introduction, this is been done perhaps because the grant was being made at the request of the Sandhanwalia Sardars, but the amount of the grant was to be deducted from their account with the Government.

1o This is somewhat interpolatory, because the reading in the original is unclear. In any case a sentiment to this effect is meant.

11 This date precedes the first payment of land revenue by Damodar, as recorded in Document XVI. The original pattās must have been demanded for the purpose of their authenticity being determined before final decisions were taken by the British authorities.

NOTES TO IV

1 This invocation is different from the alif or o of many other documents and, as we have pointed out earlier in our study of The Pindori Documents, here the three dots of the pai which follow the alif suggest that it is being used as an abbreviation for Akāl Purkh (The Immortal Being). See, thus, The Pindori Documents, No XXIX, XLII, and p. 249, note 1.

2 There is no seal on this document and only the word Sahī appears which has been thus translated. There is a possibility that this, like Document II, is issued under the authority of Raja Dhyan Singh. The Sahī is in Takri although it must be pointed out that its orthography is different from the sahī in Document II.

3 It has not been possible to identify this person. There is mention of one Kahan Singh, son of Sardar Mirza Singh of Naoshera Nangli, who was placed under the order of Sardar Desa Singh Majithia, Governor of the hills. Kahan Singh is mentioned as remaining in the service of the Majithia Chiefs and not only accompanying them in the field but filling civil offices under them. See, Lepel Griffin, p. 231. The next document adds Lala before the name of Kahan Singh and if the person in that document is the same as here, then this possible identification would not hold, because Lala as an honorific was unlikely to have been used for a Sikh.

4 It appears that it was normal practice for the original parwānā issued by the Maharaja to be followed by the parwānā of a high dignitary such as the Prime Minister which was addressed to a person by name but repeating the contents of the original and adding further exhortations and details.

5 Clearly it is Attar Singh Sandhanwalia who is meant. Gokal is mentioned as an employee of Attar Singh even though he probably served all the Sandhanwalias and this may be due to the fact that Attar Singh was the head of the Sandhanwalia family at this time, his father having died in A.D. 1827.

6 This refers probably to land that was close to or a part of the habitable area of a village. In the hills the parts of a village were often referred to as lāhars and a homestead described as a lāharī bāsī. The lāhari question was examined in some detail at the time of the first land settlement by the British. See, Gazetteer of the Kangra District, 1883-84, pp. 239-241. It is stated that even poor artisans held lāharis from the states in return for services etc.

7 This follows a standard formula which was adopted at the end of documents of this kind to lend emphasis to the instructions. This

7 cont.
appears again and again, sometimes with minor variations, in The Pindori Documents.

8 There is a gap of about six months between the last document and this one, so that the follow-up action is not immediate and the occasion for the issue of this may have been some difficulty experienced by the grantee, Gokal.

9 The use of this word here suggests that the orders originated with the Maharaja. On the other hand there is also the possibility that this word comes in as a matter of routine and "slips" from the pen of the scribe.

1o This endorsement is indication of the fact that the document is purely of a personal nature but was treated as official or, at least, as semi-official.

NOTES TO V

1 This must clearly be Ajit Singh Sandhanwalia, son of Wasawa Singh, one of the five Sandhanwalia brothers. A portrait of Ajit Singh is reproduced by W.G. Archer in his Paintings of the Sikhs, fig. 83. While that drawing is in the Victoria and Albert Museum, the British Museum also has a partly finished painting of Ajit Singh, no. 1948-1o-9-o132.

2 See, note 3 to Document IV above.

3 Ajit Singh had perhaps no official standing in this matter of issuing a document of this kind, but was generally known to be in a position of influence and hence the liberty that he takes of addressing a direct instruction to an official technically under the Governor of the hills.

4 Khālsa Jio refers fairly clearly to Ajit Singh himself and not to the Maharaja who finds mention as "the exalted Huzūr" in this very sentence. This use of Khālsa Jio is something that we have noticed in The Pindori Documents. The term was not reserved either for the Sikh brotherhood in general or for Maharaja Ranjit Singh alone.

5 This statement suggests further that Document IV which has a reference to this very matter is indeed issued by Raja Dhyan Singh.

6 The reading here is not clear, but the intention is to reassure the addressee that the grantee is in favour and to be trusted.

7 The emphasis on the quality of land confirms our impression that the land was not jāgīr land as understood in the usual sense, from which only revenues were to be collected by the grantee, but was meant to be occupied by him, so that he could live off its produce. This is partially negatived by the reference to the revenues in the next part of the sentence, but my impression is that the reference to the revenues is a slip of the pen, used as the scribe might have been to making entries like this.

8 There is vague suggestion in this phrase that Lala Kahan Singh may be assured of the support of Ajit Singh in case of any need.

9 The year is not indicated here, but perhaps it should be taken to be S. 1894 inspite of the year in the seal which is S. 1893. The seals, as we know, were used for several years after being struck. The suggestion of this being a document of S. 1894 comes from the fact that the previous Document, no. IV, is referred herein. If this is so, then this is drawn up only two days after Raja Dhyan Singh's parwānā.

1o This note did not belong to the original and has been placed as an index note by the owner of the document, perhaps Gokal himself. It appears at a point where it would show on the outside once the document is rolled up.

11 One notices the use of "Jit Singh" instead of "Ajit Singh". The name has been shortened here, as often done in popular usage, and takes the same form that appears in the inscriptions on the drawings referred to in note 1 above.

NOTES TO VI

1 It is unusual to come upon an invocatory superscription of such detail. This appears in a document bearing the seal of Gurbaksh Singh (no. XXXII) in The Pindori Documents, but on no other of the documents in that collection. Even Ajit Singh's own earlier document, no. V, uses an abbreviation.

2 It is not clear as to who has entered this on the document. It is almost certainly an entry by a Hindu and there is some possibility that the inscription is in the hand of Missar Mayya Das, the addressee, in token of his having read its contents.

3 This seal of Ajit Singh does not appear to have a date on it which would make it different from the seal he uses in Document V.

4 The word in the original is Brahmūrat, obviously an abbreviation or corruption of Brahma mūrat meaning 'the image of Brahma'. It was not uncommon to pay a compliment like this to holy men and to Brahmans. See, The letter of Aurangzeb to Mahant Anandanath (Jakhbar Document, no. VIII), in which the Mahant is addressed as "the possessor of the sublime station, Shiv murat, Guru Anand Nath Jio". In The Pindori Documents (nos. XXXVII, XL, XLVI, L, etc) titles of an elaborate kind are used to refer to Mahants.

5 It has not been possible for me to identify this official with any certainty.

6 It is interesting to notice that while the contents of the document are full of reprimand, "profuse kindness" is expressed toward the addressee. Perhaps the suggestion is that it is not the addressee but his underlings who were creating problems for the painter's family.

7 The exact nature of these imposts or customary offerings is not clear. Tambūl may possibly refer to a "voluntary contribution" to be made on occasions such as marriages, etc., in the families of officials and functionaries by the population of the village.

8 The expression used, khalish wa khijālat-i-bejā, is strong and indicates that the painter was subject to considerable harassment.

9 We know that in S. 1897 Ajit Singh Sandhanwalia, along with Lehna Singh was in the Kulu-Mandi area. It is possible that the painter was with Ajit Singh on this journey.

10 Drang, in the Mandi territory, was well-known, like Gumma, for its salt-mines.

NOTES TO VII

1 I have already published a translation of this document in, "Indian Painters of the Punjab Hills", in J. of the Royal Society of Arts, Nov. 1969. The present translation differs very slightly, but in no material respect, from the translation published earlier. The few changes offered here are because of a somewhat different reading of some Persian words.

2 It is unfortunately not clear who the writer of this letter is. The contents are secure indication that it is one of the Sandhanwalia brothers, but which one it is difficult to determine. One assumes that in personal correspondence like this the recipient knew who the writer was. Signatures do not appear almost anywhere.

3 When I published this document first, I was of the view that this Lehna Singh was one of the Sandhanwalia brothers, mostly because of the use of "dear brother" in the address. It appears now to me more likely, however, that "dear brother" is not literally meant and that the addressee may be none other than Lehna Singh Majithia, the Governor of the hills. I am inclined to this view because of the implication that the addressee is in an official position to dispose of the matter and this could then be the nāzim or Governor. The filial sentiment is thus more a pleasantry than a description of actual relationship.

4 It is interesting to see that nearly one half of the writing space is taken up by the address and the opening sentences: the contents have partly to be pushed into the margin!

5 I have not been able to get any information about this incident from the members of the family.

6 The respectful way in which the town of Kangra is referred to is worthy of notice. This comes from the sacredness of the temple of the Goddess in that town and one sees a parallel here to "Srī Amritsar Jio" which is used for that city in references.

7 The reading here is not clear at all and perhaps the translation only approximates to the sense of the original.

8 From this it appears that Chhajju himself may not have been in the service of the Sandhanwalia Chiefs. It is only Harkhu who is mentioned and the letter of recommendation may have been written at the asking of Harkhu on behalf of his brother.

9 There is unfortunately no date on this document. Its placing here is somewhat arbitrary.

NOTES TO VIII

1 I am grateful to Sri V.S. Suri for identifying for me this signature in French spellings by the Maharaja. These are, of course, of great interest and I have found them on another document relating to a grant of lands to the Mahant of Dhyanpur, the large Vaishnava gaddi in Gurdaspur District.

2 The relatively large number of seals here is something which characterizes the document from the period of Maharaja Sher Singh. See, thus, The Pindori Documents, no. L. Apparently Sher Singh introduced revised procedures in official matters like this.

3 Sher Singh uses the formula "Satgur Sahai" in some of the seals in The Pindori Documents (no. XLVIII, L), but here the formula appears to be "akal sahai", even though the impression of the seal is not very good.

4 It is interesting to see that this seal bearing the date S. 1887 is still in use and is being affixed on this document of eleven years later.

5 The titles or honorifics used for Lehna Singh seem to have come down from the period of the great Maharaja and, at least, in this case, reflect accurately the opinion held of this able Majithia Sardar by both Ranjit Singh and Sher Singh.

6 The details of the jāgīr given here fit in once again with the general care with which the patta has been inscribed, endorsed, entered, etc.

7 As remarked in the introduction, Sher Singh reclaims Gokal for himself from the Sandhanwalia Sardars. This may as much be an indication of his own interest in painting (on which we have other information also) as of the fact that things were not going well between the Maharaja and the Sandhanwalias.

8 This was apparently the office in which the records like this enrolment were maintained.

9 Cf. the large number of similar endorsement entries on no. L of The Pindori Documents. Unfortunately, because of the high degree of stylization in the writing, it has not been possible to decipher all the entries precisely.

1o This, undoubtely, is the famous keeper of accounts of the Sikh court, also known as'Raja' Dina Nath. He was a familiar figure at the court and appears in a series of woodcuts of the second half of the 19th century among the "twelve heroes of the Sikhs" as Mr. Archer calls

1o cont.

them. See, his <u>Paintings of the Sikhs</u>, fig. 1o8-111. He almost always appears either reading from or writing on a paper held in his hand.

NOTES TO IX

1 As indicated in note 74 to the introduction, Bawa Lachhman Singh was a "confidential servant" of the Majithias. The Umadat-ut-Tawarikh, vol. IV, p. 82, has an entry of the 28th of December 1839 mentioning "Baba Lachhman Singh, a reliable person of Sirdar Majithia" presenting himself at the court and giving an account of the arrival of the Commander in Chief of the British forces in Malsian.

2 The chaudhari, according to Irfan Habib (pp. 126-127, 289-294), was usually a zamindar himself and occupied a crucial position in the machinery of revenue collection. This position was usually hereditary even though an imperial order was necessary to legalize the appointment of a new chaudhari. See, The Jakhbar Documents, pp.155-156, note 4 and the Pindori Documents, p. 116, note 13.

3 It has not been possible for me to identify Chaudhari Chuhar more fully.

4 It is significant that for the same grant of land, Document VIII uses the word jāgīr whereas this document uses muāfi (and jāgīr). Quite obviously the two are regarded, in this context at least, as interchangeable terms, a point which has been made in the introduction.

5 The impression from the introduction of a crop and a date like this is likely to be that the muāfi was to be effective only from this date. We know, however, from our general view of these documents, that the grant continued to be enjoyed, but the crop and the year were mentioned as a matter of course, when a document was being drawn up.

6 This document represents follow-up action on the previous document. While Sher Singh's parwānā is issued at Amritsar, Bawa Lachhman Singh probably takes local action consequent upon orders from above.

7 There is a gap only of nine days between the issue of the Mahāraja's parwānā (Document VIII) and this document, indicating that action was swift and decisive.

NOTES TO X

1 This is the same seal that appears on the previous document.

2 The Gazetteer of the Kangra District, 1883/84 (p. 219), gives us some information on Bhagat Boghu Shah, while mentioning the fact that kārdārs were frequently transferred and as a rule did not stay in power for more than three years. "Instances have occurred, such for example as Boghu Shah at Kangra, when the kārdār has held this position for fiteen or twenty years; but he was a personal favourite with Lehna Singh, and owed his protracted tenure to his chief's support."

3 The contents of this document are much the same as those of Document IX with the difference that these two are issued in the name of two different persons. This is obviously because the land in the taaluqas of Rihlu and Haripur fell in two differrent parganas, the officials of which had to be addressed separately.

4 There is no mention of a muāfi here and only the word jāgīr is used. Quite obviously, however, this fact is not significant, for the two words are being used almost synonymously in these documents.

5 Contrary to the impression about the honesty or popularity of Bhagat Boghu Shah that one gains from the Gazetteer of the Kangra District (see note 2 above), these sentences (which do not appear in the previous document) suggest that Bawa Lachhman Singh felt the need to issue emphatic instructions in this case.

6 The date of the issue of this Document is the same as of Document IX. Obviously, with the issue of this, action was completed in the matter of the grants in both the taaluqas.

7 The sense of this sentence is not clear. It may refer, on the one hand, to Gokal being permitted to retain the parwānā for future use, or the reference here may be to Bhagat Boghu Shah being asked to issue a parwānā of his own to Gokal to re-assert the fact of the grants.

8 We are familiar with the usage of this word from The Jakhbar Documents and The Pindori Documents. It indicates "the end" to guard against the possibility of any later, unauthorized additions to the documents. Steingass defines it simply as "a mark fixed to public writings by the magistrate or any principal officer", but this does not bring out the significance of its appearance at the end of a formal document. See, further, The Jakhbar Documents, p. 112, note 6, and The Pindori Documents, p. 8o, note 3, p. 3o5, note 1o. This is the only one of the documents in the present collection in which baiz appears.

NOTES TO XI

1 This appears to be a substitute for the sahī which has been noticed on some other documents. The purport of this inscription is simply to indicate, as in the case of sahī, that the document has been drawn up correctly as per the intentions of the issuing authority.

2 Even though there is no specific indication in the seal, it is almost certain that this seal is of Sardar Lehna Singh Majithia. The other possibility that it could be of Sardar Lehna Singh Sandhanwalia is perhaps to be discounted in view of the contents which are much more formal than they would have been if it were a recommendatory letter etc..

3 Even though the reading in the original is closer to "Lohku Shah" it is almost certain that the addressee is Boghu Shah whom we know of as being the kardar of Kangra. See, note 2, to Document X; above.

4 There is no mention of land in the original and only a cash amount is indicated. While, in all probability, this document refers only to a cash annual grant, a naqad jāgīr, there is a faint possibility that mention of land was omitted inadvertently.

5 We know of a painter of this name from Kangra from an inscription at the back of a painting in the Chandigarh Museum. Very little else is known about him. A painter of this very name, we know from the records of the priests at Haridwar, belonged to the village Chari, now in the Kangra District.

6 It is not possible to determine which "Raja Sahib" is meant here. But fairly clearly a former Rajput ruler of a hill state is alluded to.

7 It would have been of great interest to learn why the grant to Fauju was being transferred to Harkhu, for we know very little of how and why grants were withdrawn and patronage transferred. There is the likelihood that Fauju died in this year, but the document does not make any mention of this.

8 While there is nothing explicit to indicate that Lehna Singh was personally interested in transferring this grant to Harkhu, and while the orders are being executed in the name of the Maharaja, there is some possibility that Lehna Singh had enrolled Harkhu in his own service. One cannot, of course, go in a case like this beyond assumption.

NOTES TO XII

1 It is not possible to determine who the writer of this invocation is. Clearly this is not a part of the document, but a later superscription. Cf. a similar superscription in Document VI above.

2 A departure is made herein from the usual practice of making the address elaborate. Perhaps the tone of the letter arises from the circumstance to which the contents point.

3 This must be the extent of land referred to in Documents VIII, IX and X, where the grant of this amount is in the name of Gokal. It is possible that there were no separate grants for the brothers and the assumption was that it was the family which received the grant rather than an individual.

4 In the reference to the "exalted parwana", there is some indication that the issuing authority is a high official, perhaps at Lahore, rather than a local official at the pargana or taaluqa headquaters.

5 There is no inkling anywhere of the cause leading to this seeming tension between brothers, but there is clear suggestion that the property is to be divided. A situation in which at first things went smoothly and the grant was held in common, and trouble developed between the brothers later, is not difficult to conceive.

6 This, once again, draws attention to the fact that the grant implied the actual occupation and cultivation of the land received by the painters in grant. If the intention of the "jāgīr" terms was for the painters only to claim revenue to this extent from a marked area of land, this insistence on the quality of the land would be somewhat devoid of point.

7 The use of the word aimma here, as has been noted before, is certainly of interest. One notices once again that the produce from the land is as much in question as the land itself.

8 Unfortunately there is no date to this document, and it has been placed here because of the reference to land worth Rupees 225 here which must follow documents VIII, IX, and X.

NOTES TO XIII

1 It has not been possible to identify this person. All one can conclude perhaps is that he was a functionary at the court in Lahore, but not of a very high rank.

2 The sense in the original is unfortunately not clear. This may not necessarily refer to any British "sahib", for the word was used for any superior also.

3 The reference to <u>tankhwāh</u> is interesting because it implies payment in cash for the most part. Chhajju may have been enrolled on cash terms, possibly in addition to the grant of land that stood already in his name or that of his family.

4 "A storeroom, a wardrobe; chambers in which objects of curiosity or value, not in daily request, are kept." (Wilson's <u>Glossary</u>, p. 525). Here, however, the word may have the sense of the treasury from which the salaries were issued.

5 The term <u>bandā-i-dargāh</u> is found used repeatedly in Mughal documents, as much for very highly placed officials as for the lower functionaries.

6 It has not been possible to identify this person, but one can take it that he was a <u>chaudhari</u> whom Chhajju knew in the hills and whom he got to write this recommendatory note on his behalf.

NOTES TO XIV

1 This is in a different hand than the inscription that follows it immediately. Obviously, the document passed through the hands of two different officials both of whom put these "signs" in token of their having seen the document and taken action on it, or at least noted its contents.

2 A Mutasaddi is "a writer, a clerk". While the document is addressed to the group of Mutasaddis of this office, obviously the matter would have been handled by one person who dealt with this specific category of service-enrolments.

3 Cf. the reference to the Daftar-i-Mu'allah in Document VIII, also. It emerges clearly from these that records of enrolment were kept in that office.

4 The full details of the identification of Gokal, with his parentage etc. and the place of this residence fully indicated, appear only in this document which, for all its insignificant size, is perhaps the most formal of all in this collection.

5 From this it is not to be understood that Gokal was entering service for the first time now. We know from the other documents that he was already in service. Perhaps it is a changed circumstance, like Gokal coming and temporarily settling down in the court, which is the occasion for the issue of revised terms of this engagement.

6 There is no indication for what period is this quantity to be issued. Perhaps the measure relates to the issue each day which would make it a handsome amount.

7 Unfortunately the reading here is by no means free of doubt, but if the amount mentioned is indeed Rupee 3o per mensem, then the payment by current standards was clearly good.

8 Once again the reading is doubtful, although less doubtful than in the case of the cash salary. Neither the area of the land nor its annual value is indicated and perhaps the assumption is that the land already in conferment is to continue to be enjoyed by Gokal in addition to the other facilities.

9 Unfortunately, the Khalsa Darbar Records which must have other entries relating to painters etc. have not been fully published. There is only an index by Prof. Sitaram Kohli which contains no clear information on this specific point.

1o While the formula used is mulāhizā shud meaning "examined", the meaning is that the orders contained in the document have been carried out and the name of Gokal entered in the relevant record.

NOTES TO XV

1 This endorsement on the face of the document is to indicate that the contents have been noted and the instructions carried out. It is difficult to ascertain in whose hand this note is.

2 Ranjodh Singh, half-brother of Sardar Lehna Singh Majithia, had at this time taken over the administration of the hills after the departure of Lehna Singh to places of pilgrimage in the east. This seal appears also on other documents in the hills that I have had occasion to see. Clearly his coming to power neccessitated the reissue of practically all grants.

3 It has not been possible to identify Wazir Karam Singh firmly. It is not unlikely that he was not really a "minister", but had only a family title if he came from a Rajput family that had served the former rulers of the hills. We have a reference to one Karam Singh, _Thanedar_ of the Fort of Kangra, presenting himself before Maharaja Sher Singh on April 11, 1843, during his visit to Rambagh near the Fort of Kangra. The _Umdat-ut-Tawarikh_ (Vol. IV, p. 225) mentions a _sarwarna_ and offering of Rupees 5oo "by way of entertainment" by Karam Singh to the Maharaja. A "Wazir Karam Singh of Mandi" is listed among the _jāgīrdārs_ of Kangra proper in the _Gazetteer of the Kangra District_, 1883-84, p. 137. He held jagir valued at Rupees 1,612.

4 The convention of mentioning the half of the principal amount in question in addition to the amount itself was clearly a safeguard against errors and tampering with of the figures.

5 This _khālsa Jio_ refers fairly clearly to Ranjodh Singh himself even as "the exalted Sarkar" refers to the ruler at Lahore. The usage is interesting in the context of the general impression that only the Maharaja was referred to in these terms.

6 This may be indication that the Gurmukhi note on the top may be in the hand of Ranjodh Singh himself and may have been placed there instead of the more common "sahī".

7 This is a crossing on the river Sutlej about six miles from Phillaur.

8 While the document specifically relates to Gokal and mentions the value of the land held by him as Rupees 1oo, this detail brings in the land worth Rupees 5o per annum to Chhajju also (thus giving a total of Rupees 15o) in order to avoid any confusion in the matter. This is not apparently the whole of the land, some of which must have been located in a different _pargana_ than the one over which Karam Singh had control. No reduction in the grant to Gokal need be concluded from this document.

NOTES TO XVI

1 The use of the seal of a local functionary during the British period is of interest. There is no invocation in the seal and it is not unlikely that it was made in the new, relatively "secular" regime. The position of Hadi Hussain Khan is not indicated by anything in the document.

2 One notices that there is no superscription or invocation at the top of this document or of the three that follow it. Only the date of its issue is given.

3 Wilson's Glossary, p. 318-319, describes a mahal as: "A province, a district, ...; a division of a Taālluk, or district, yielding revenue according to assessment. In the language of the Regulations a Mahal, or Mehal, is called an estate, and is defined as any parcel or parcels of land which may be separately assessed with the public revenue; ..." For Mahal, also see, The Jakhbar Documents, pp. 66, 67, note 7. It is in this document for the first time in this collection that this word occurs.

4 It has not been possible, unfortunately, to decipher the figure preceding this word in the document.

5 Steingass describes a tahwildar as a "cash-keeper; treasurer; custodian". It is possible that the office of a tahwildar was a new introduction in the Kangra area by the British.

6 One notices that the name of the crop for which land revenue is being collected here is not indicated. It is quite likely that this is only a rounded, initial payment to be kept in trust pending final decision on the quantum of revenue from this land.

7 This sign al-abd or abduh, as abbreviation of anā'abduh-hu meaning "(I am) his servant or slave", appears on numerous Mughal documents. Wilson's Glossary, p. 2, notices that abd was "frequently prefixed in affectation of humility to the official signatures of native officers, whether Hindus or Mohammedans; and in law papers it is sometimes prefixed to the name of each subscribing witness".

8 Wilson's Glossary defines siyāhah, p. 481, as: "An account book, an inventory, a list: it is especially applied in Hindustan to the daily ledger or account-book of the receipts and disbursements of a village or estate, specifying all sums received, whether regular or miscellaneous, and all items of disbursement, whether customary or incidental; ..." Also see, for siyāhah, The Jakhbar Documents, pp. 138-139, note 22 and The Pindori Documents, p. 99, note 15. A siyāhahnawīs would be one who make entries in the account books etc.

NOTES TO XVII

1 There is one entry which is inscribed across the face of this document on top, but I have not been able to read this.

2 The mention of the crop and the year makes a departure from document XVI. The indication here is that the amount of revenue due from Damodar has been determined, something that receives further support from the exact amount down to annas and pies that is mentioned.

3 The reading is not clear, but is perhaps muzabtā or mazbūta. While neither of these is a recognized derivation from zabt kardan, "to confiscate, sieze, etc.", the general sense of the situation perhaps warrants this translation.

4 "A village, understanding by that term one or more clusters of habitations, and all the lands belonging to their proprietory inhabitants: ...." (Wilson's Glossary, p. 336). The unit under this name was probably not defined under the Sikh regime and is introduced on the earlier Mughal pattern perhaps by the British.

5 This is the same as Rajol. Even today this diminutive form of the name is frquently used.

6 The reading of this word is by no means free of doubt. If the word does read sūd, "interest", then it may relate to the interest falling due on the principal amount in the event of late payment.

NOTES TO XVIII

1 The seal of Sayyad Hadi Hussain Khan does not appear on this document, the only one of the four of this group in which this is the case.

2 Land revenue was collected in instalments from the very beginning of the British rule in these parts. The months in which the instalments were collected varied in the different parts of the Kangra District. See <u>Gazetteer of the Kangra District</u>, 1883-84, p. 231.

3 The amount of revenue of the <u>kharīf</u> crop can be seen to be much higher than on the <u>rabī</u> crop. This was a usual situation in India. The revenue demand for the <u>kharīf</u> crop was sometimes as much as three times the demand for the <u>rabī</u>. Some idea of the relative importance of these crops can be had from the figures for the district of Kangra (<u>Gazetteer of the Kangra District</u>, p. 231) which mentions the amount of Rupees 54,926 for the <u>rabī</u> crop as revenue and Rupees 1,77,167 for the <u>kharīf</u> crop.

4 The use of the word <u>muāfi</u> for small grants such as these was much more common than the use of the word <u>jāgīr</u> in British papers, relating to these cases.

5 The reading of this word in the original is much closer to <u>sarak</u> (road?) rather than to <u>sūd</u> as in Document XVII. In this connection one thinks of a road fund which was levied by the British in addition to the other levies officially fixed such as <u>lambardār's</u> fees, <u>patwāri</u>'s fees etc.

NOTES TO XIX

1 In this seal, Hadi Hussain Khan describes himself as a munshi rather than as "Sayyad" as in the earlier seal. This is in all probability with reference to his official designation or status.

2 The instalment referred to here is the second part or instalment of revenue due on the kharīf crop itself. The amount was split up for the convenience of the cultivators, a practice which continues, Sri Chandulal says, even today.

3 In the phraseology of these documents one notices the gradual emergence of a standard form which then is followed as a matter of routine.

4 The addition of this amount of Rupees 43, one Anna and 6 Pies to the Rupees 42 and 2 Annas gives the total amount of Rupees 85, three Annas and 6 Pies for the kharīf crop in all.

NOTES TO XX

1 I have published this document earlier in the Journal of the Royal Society of Arts, Nov. 1969, where only the first part has, however, been translated and included.

2 My impression earlier was that this petition was addressed to the Maharani of Garhwal, because Saudagar did work at Garhwal for some time. I am, however, inclined more now to the view that the addressee may be the Maharani of Chamba, the Queen mother, who looked after the affairs of Chamba state as a regent after her son Sri Singh succeeded to the throne of Chamba in 1844 at the age of five. It was the 'Kangra Rani' of Chamba who was carrying on the administration and the petition would thus be appropriately addressed to her.

3 This is the conventional manner in which Rajputs of noble rank were greeted. Jai deyā as a salutation was peculiar to the hills and could not be offered to persons other than of the prescribed class or rank of Rajputs.

4 Saudagar uses for himself the Persian word ghulām and not chākar which was more commonly employed.

5 If this document is addressed to the Queen mother of Chamba, then this would be a reference to Charat Singh (1808-1844) whose interest in painting is known.

6 One is led to comparing these terms to those on which Gokal was engaged at ~~the~~ Lahore court. See Document XIV.

7 This corresponds to the oral information given by the present day painters. Apparently the rewards were handsome and bore a relationship to the quality of work presented by a painter. The painters often thought of the land and rations etc. more as retainer than as full payment for their work for a court.

8 One finds an echo of the plaint of Shiba to Maharaja Sansar Chand in these words of Saudagar.

9 Apparently this document only contains a draft of the petition. This portion represents some amendments or improvements in the contents of the petition which may have been suggested by someone more conversant with the suave tenor of the court. One notices that the tone of these amendments is of even more humility and flattery.

APPENDICES

Table 1

The Family of Ranjit Singh

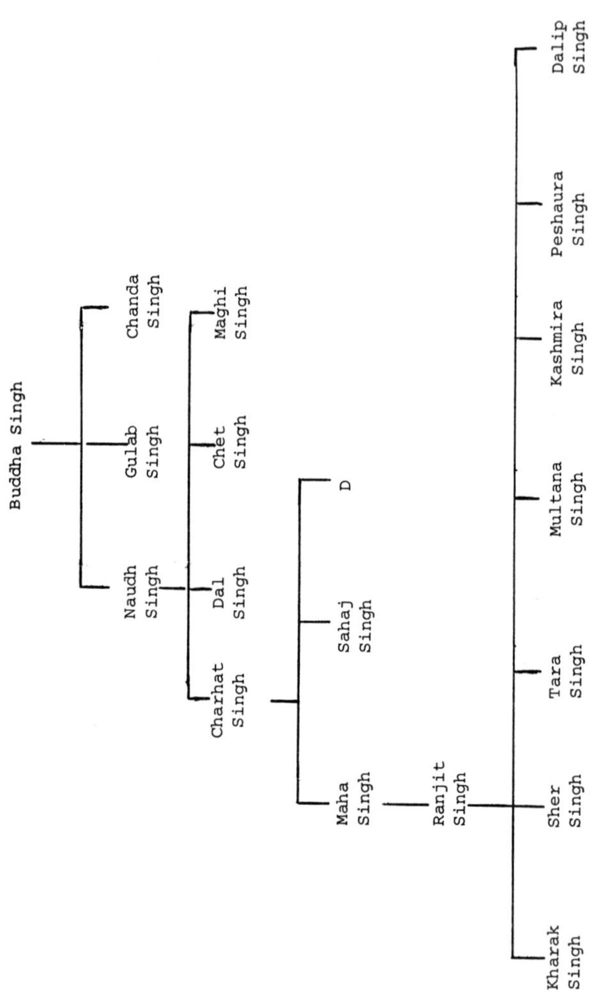

Table II

Genealogical table of the Sandhanwalia Family

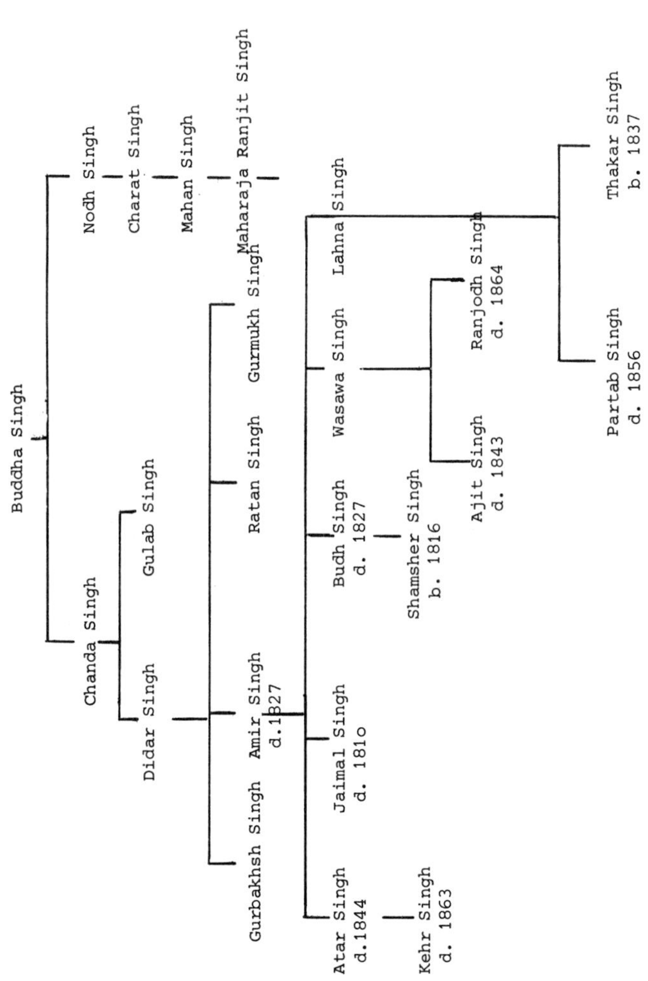

Table III

The dates in the Vikrama Samvat used in the following documents as given in the second column correspond to the dates in the Christian Calendar given in the third column.

Document	Vikrama Samvat date	Christian Calendar date
I	31 Asuj, 1882	14 October, 1825
II	23 Magh, 1882	31 January, 1826
III	9 Magh, 1893	19 January, 1837
IV	23 Sawan, 1894	5 August, 1837
V	25 Sawan, 1894	7 August, 1837
VI	25 Asuj, 1897	8 October, 184o
VIII	18 Maghar, 1898	1 December, 1841
IX	27 Maghar, 1898	1o December, 1841
X	27 Maghar, 1898	1o December, 1841
XI	2o Asuj, 1899	4 October, 1842
XIV	1o Jeth, 19oo	21 May, 1843
XV	16 Magh, 19o2	24 January 1845

SELECT BIBLIOGRAPHY

Anand, Mulk Raj, 'Painting under the Sikhs', Mārg, Vol. VII, N. 2 (1954).

Archer, W.G., Paintings of the Sikhs, HMSO, London 1966.

Archer, W.G., Indian Paintings from the Punjab Hills, 2 Vols., London 1973.

Cunningham, J.D., A History of the Sikhs, S. Chand & Co., Delhi, Lucknow and Jullundur 1955.

Dosanj, S.S., and Uttam Singh, Rao, 'A dated Janam Sakhi of Guru Nanak'. Roopa Lekha, Vol.XXXIX, N. 1.

Goetz, H., 'Some court portraits of the Pahari School in Dutch Collections'. JISOA (1933), Vol. I, N. 2.

Goswamy, B.N., and Grewal, J.S., The Mughals and the Jogis of Jakhbar. Simla 1967.

Goswamy, B.N., 'Pahari Painting: The Family as the basis of style'. Mārg, Vol. XXI, N. 4 (September 1968).

Goswamy, B.N., 'Indian Painters of the Punjab Hills'. Journal of the Royal Society of Arts, November 1969.

Goswamy, B.N., and Grewal, J.S., The Mughal and the Sikh Rulers and the Vaishnavas of Pindori. Simla 1969.

Goswamy, B.N., 'Sikh Painting: An Analysis of some aspects of Patronage'. Oriental Art, Vol. XV, 1969.

Goswamy, B.N., 'Painters in Chamba: A Discussion of the Attra Inscription'. Lalit Kalā, N. 15.

Goswamy, B.N., 'Painting in Chamba: A Study of new Documents'. Asian Review, Vol. II, N. 1.

Goswamy, B.N., 'The Artist Family of Rajol: New Light on an Old Problem'. Roopa Lekha, Vol. XXXV.

Goswamy, B.N., 'A Painter's Letter to his Royal Patron: An Old Takri Document'. JAOS, Vol. 86, N. 2.

Gazetteer of the Kangra District, Vol. I, Calcutta 1883-84.

Griffin, Sir Lepel, Chiefs and Families of Note in the Punjab. Vol. I, Lahore 19o9.

Gupta, H.R., A History of the Sikhs (1739-1799). Vol. I, Minerva Book Shop, Simla 1952.

Gupta, H.R., A History of the Sikhs. Vol. II, Lahore 1944.

Gupta, S.N., 'The Sikh School of Painting'. Rupam (1922), Vol. III, N. 12.

Hutchison, J., and Vogel, J.Ph., History of the Panjab Hill States. 2 Vols., Lahore 1933.

Irfan Habib, The Agrarian System of Mughal India. Asia Publishing House, Bombay 1963.

Khushwant Singh, Ranjit Singh (Maharaja of the Punjab). George Allen and Unwin, London 1962.

Khushwant Singh, 'Guru Nanak in Janam Sakhi Paintings'. Times of India Annual, 1971.

Prem Singh Hoti Mardan, Maharaja Sher Singh. (Punjabi) Lahore Book Shop, Ludhiana, n.d.

Randhawa, M.S., 'Kangra Artists', Art and Letters, 1955.

Randhawa, M.S., 'Sikh Painting', Roopalekha, Vol. XXXIX.

Randhawa, M.S., 'Two Punjabi Artists of the 19th century - Kehar Singh and Kapur Singh', Chhavi, 1971.

Sinha, Narendra Krishna, Ranjit Singh. University of Calcutta 1933.

Steingass, F., Persian-English Dictionary. 4th edition. London 1957.

Suri, V.S., (ed.) Umdat-ul-Tawarikh. (Daftar III) S. Chand & Co., Delhi 1961.

Suri, V.S., (ed.) Umdat-ul-Tawarikh. (Daftar IV) Chandigarh 1972.

Waheeduddin, Fakir Syed, The Real Ranjit Singh. Karachi 1965.

Wilson, H.H., A Glossary of Judicial & Revenue Terms of British India & c. London 1855.

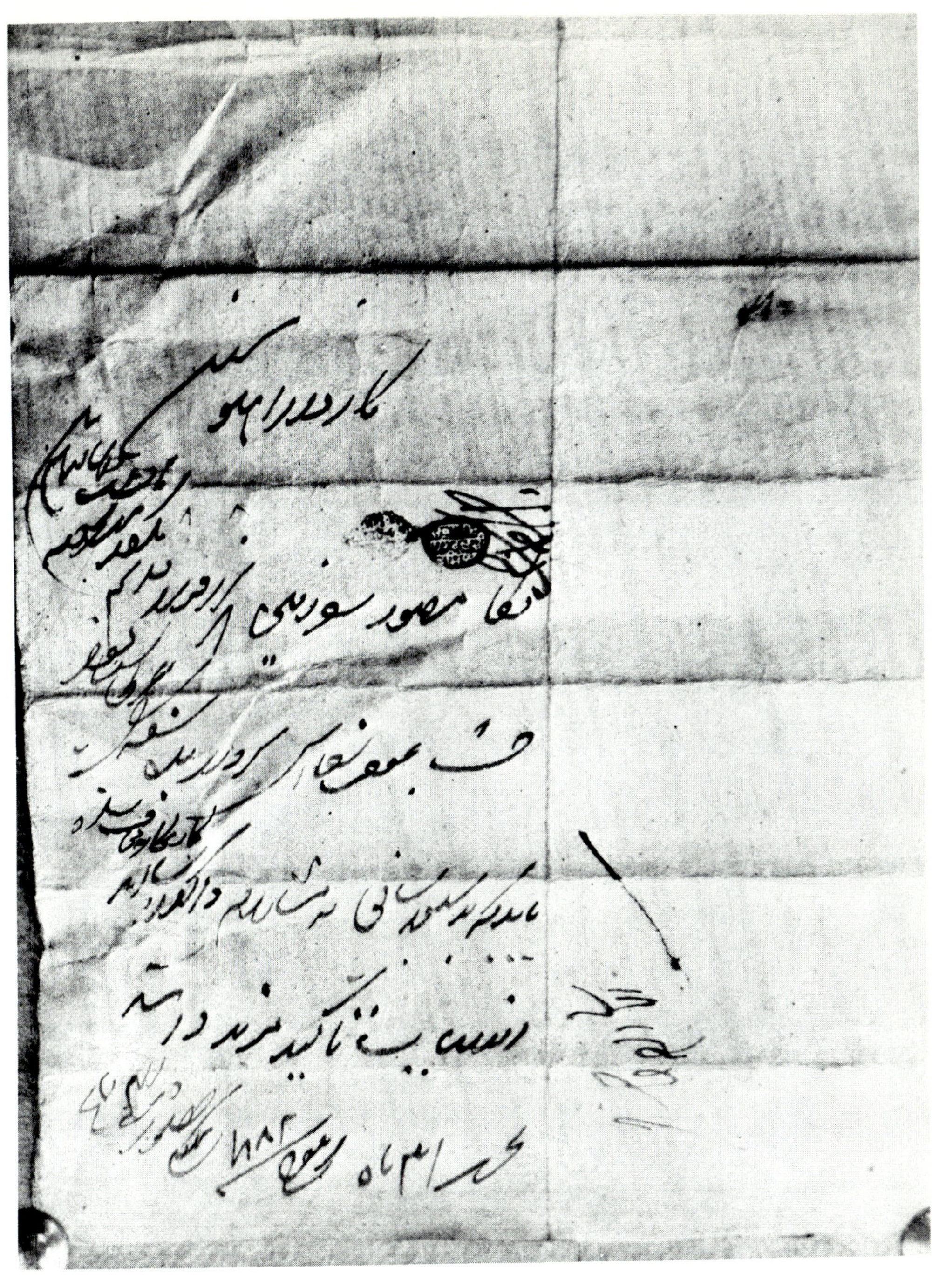

I : 19 x 13,5

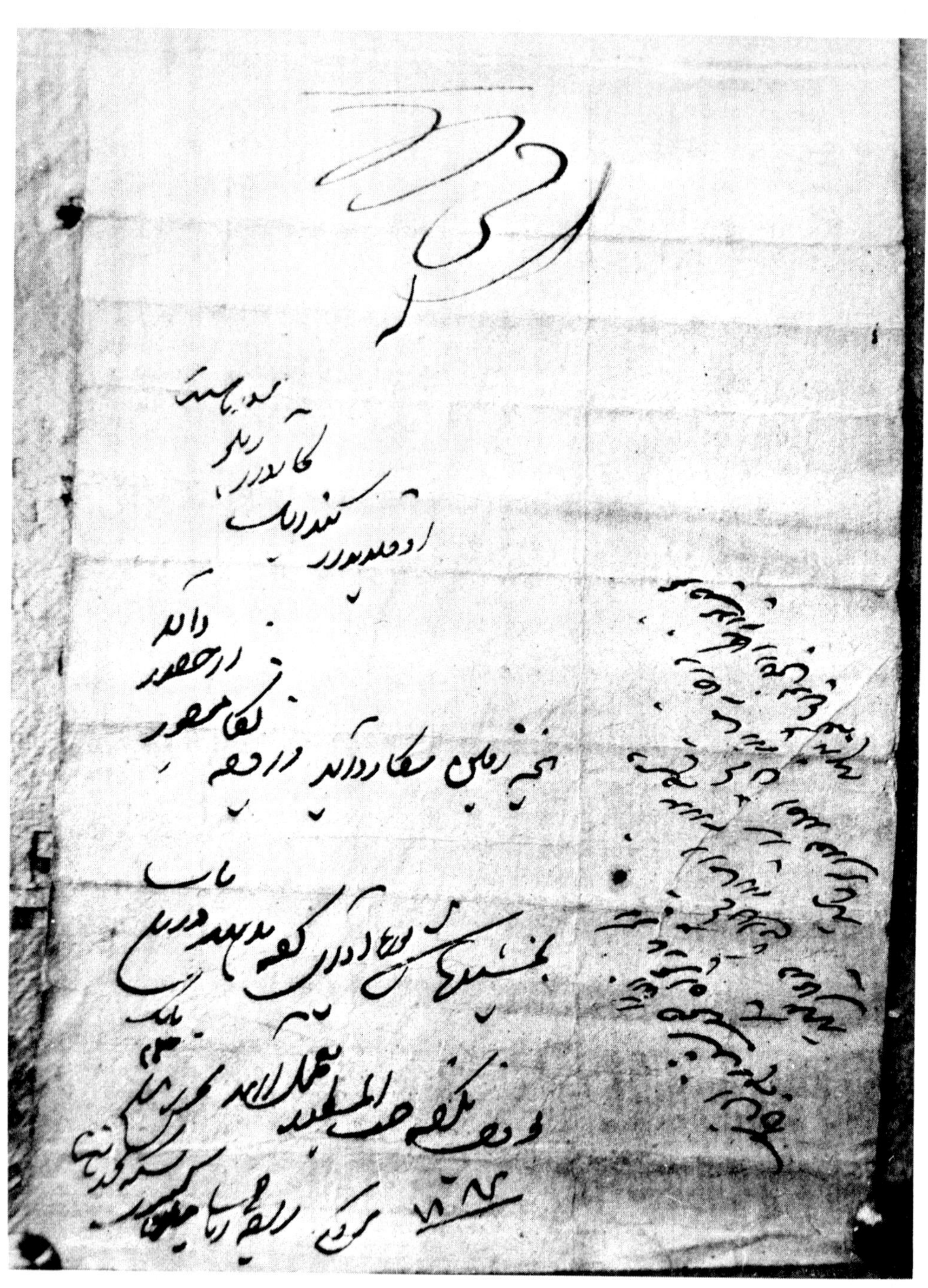

II : 22 x 13

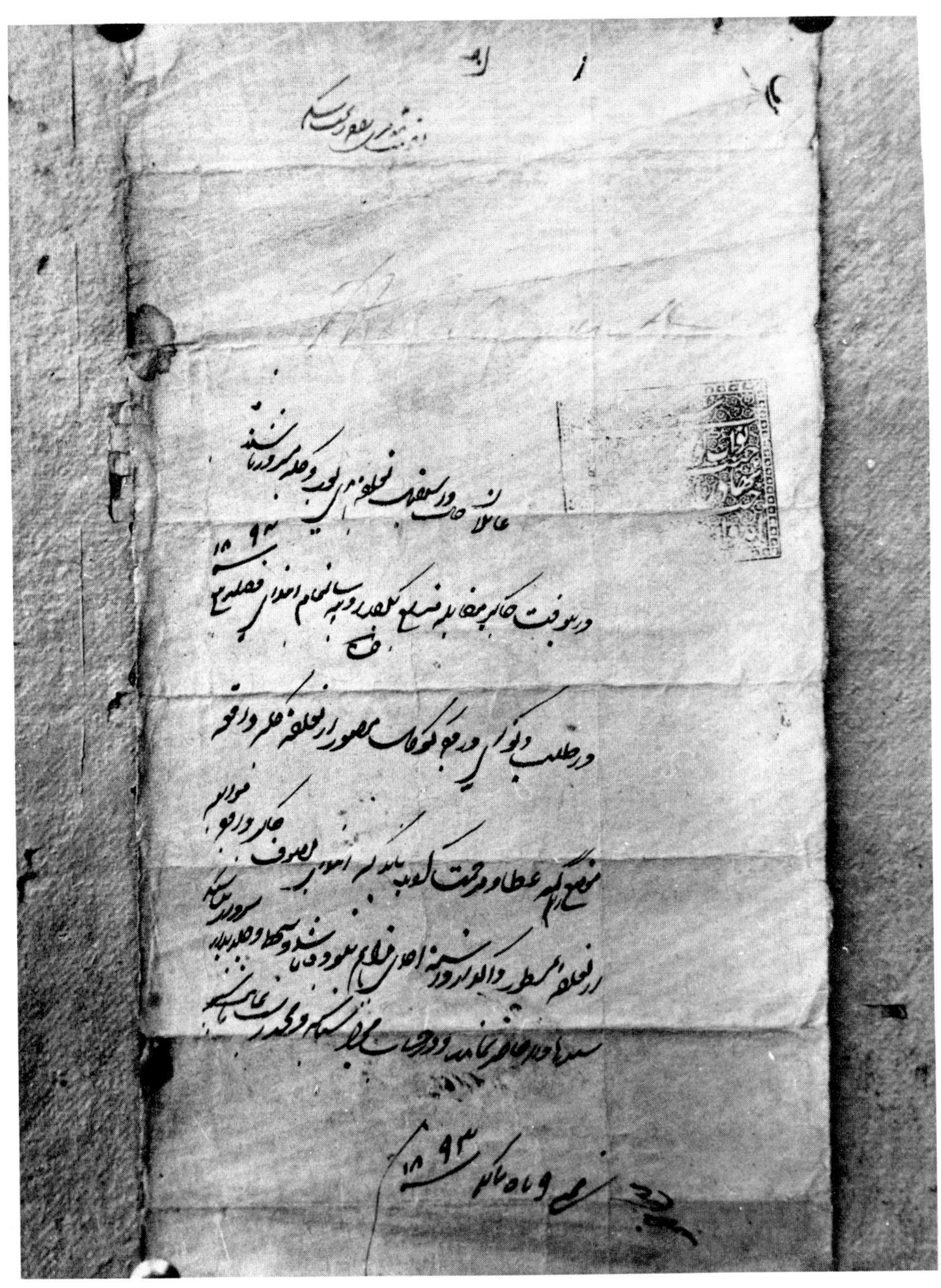

III : 3o x 16,5

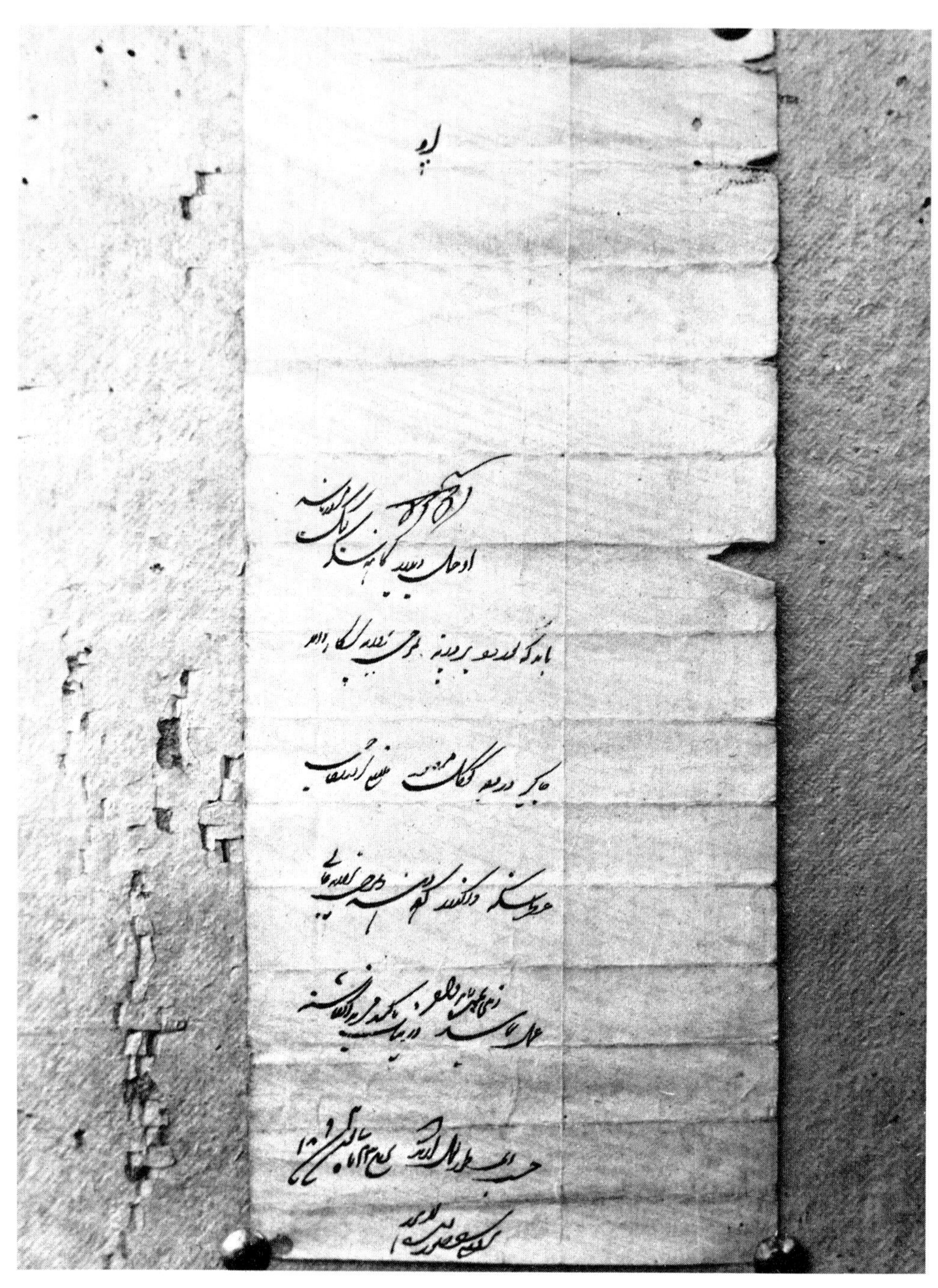

IV : 31,5 x 13,5

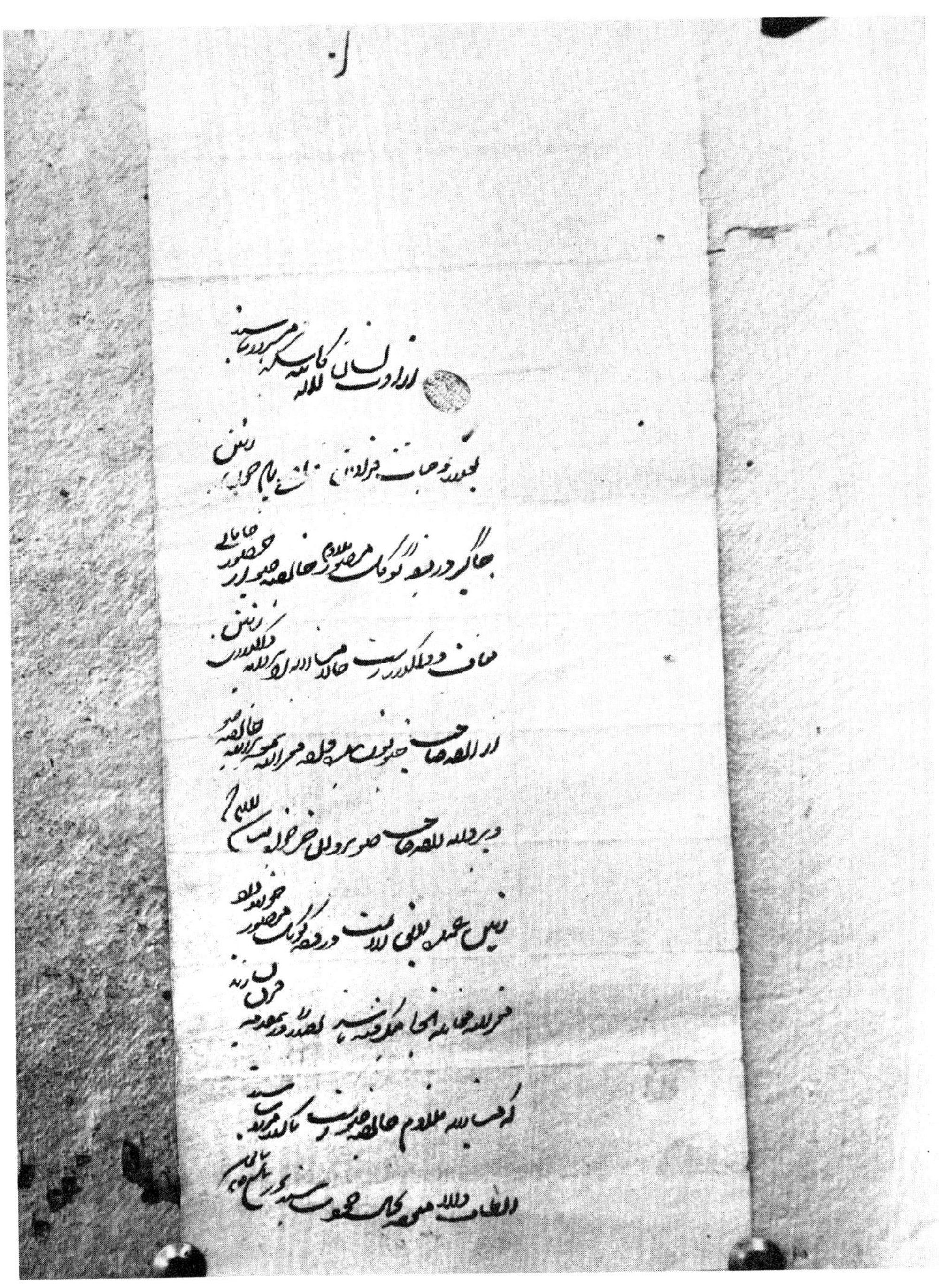

V : 31 x 13

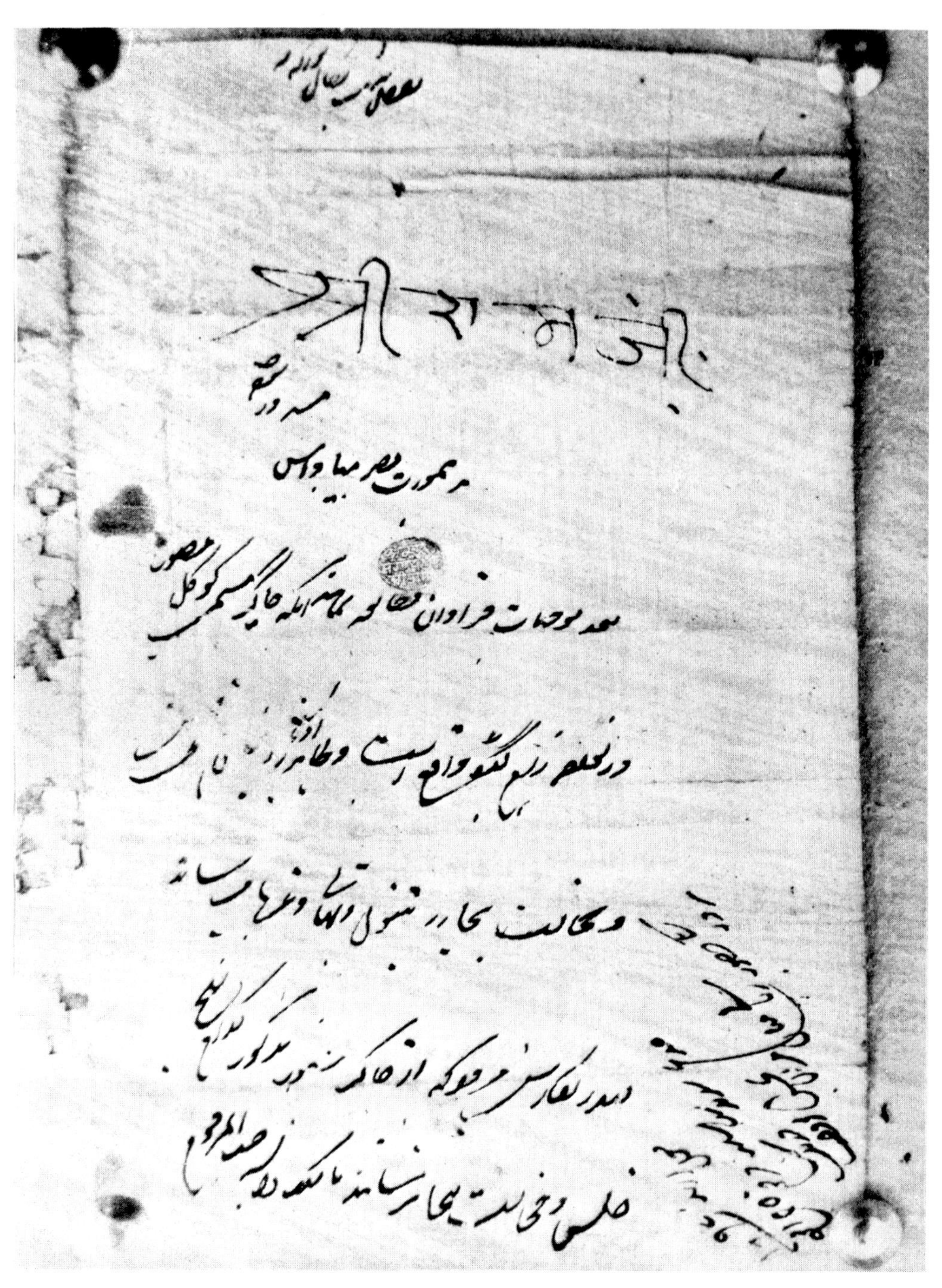

VI : 2o x 13,5

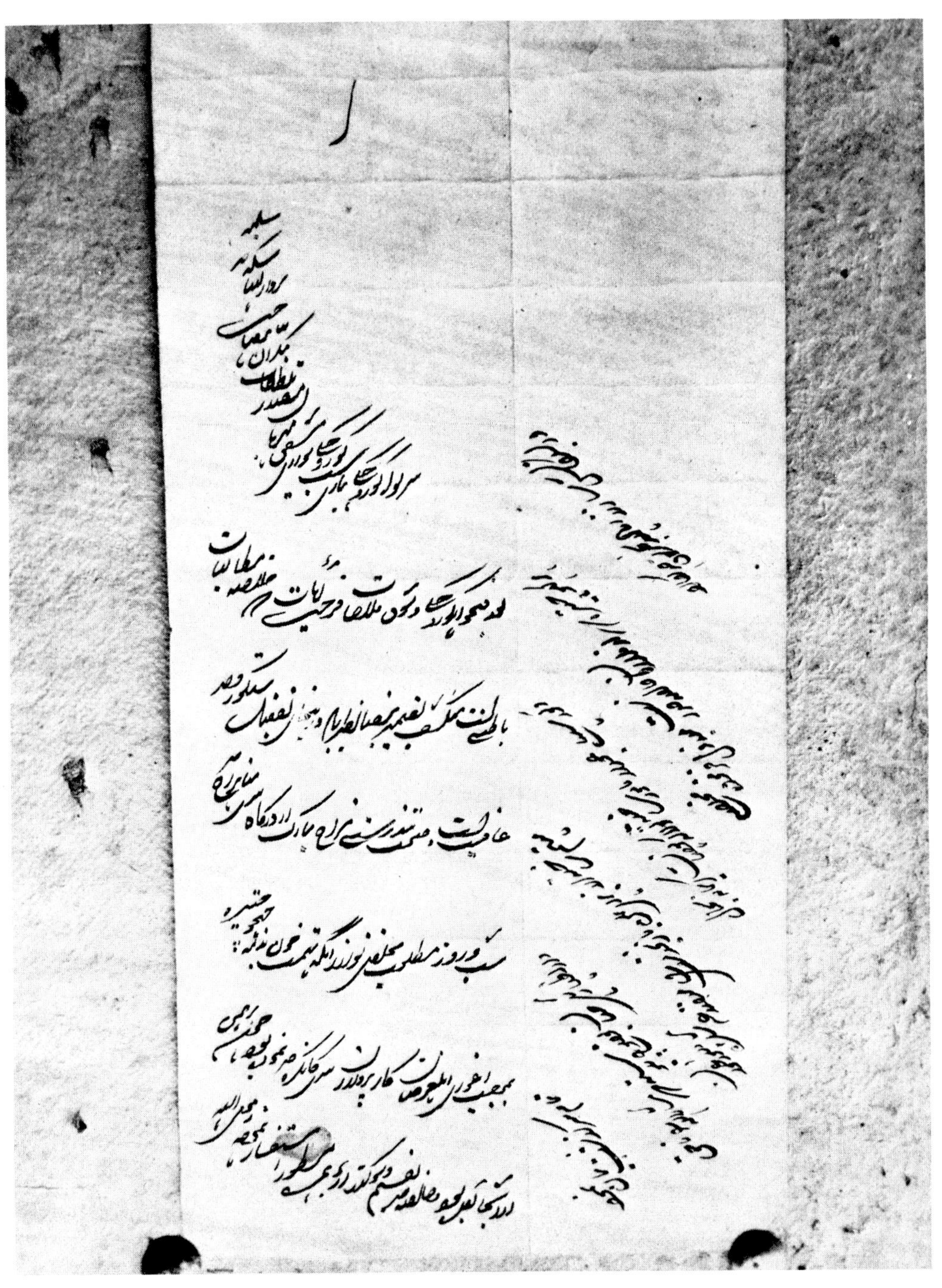

VII : 31,5 x 13,5

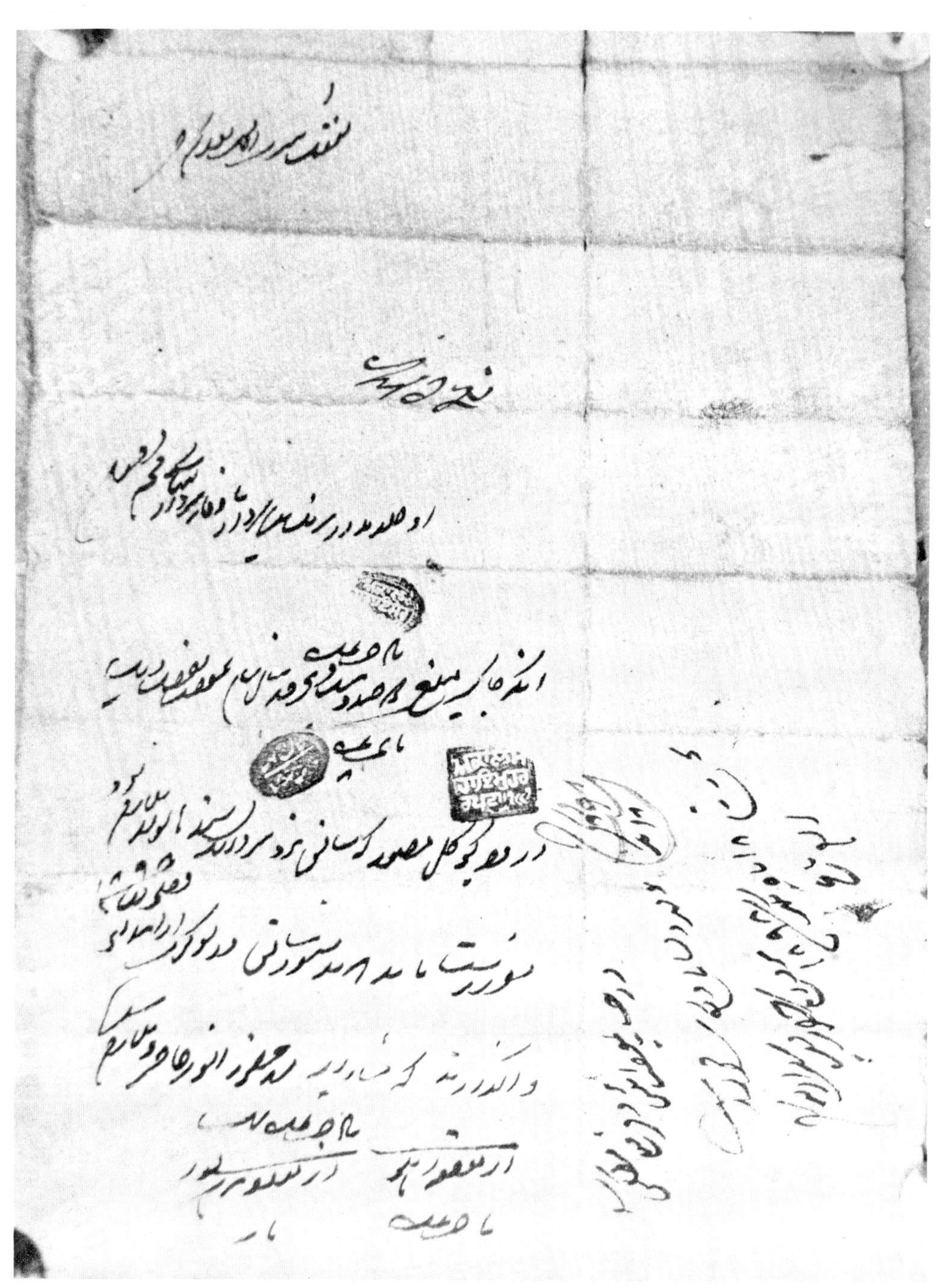

VIII : 17,5 x 12,5

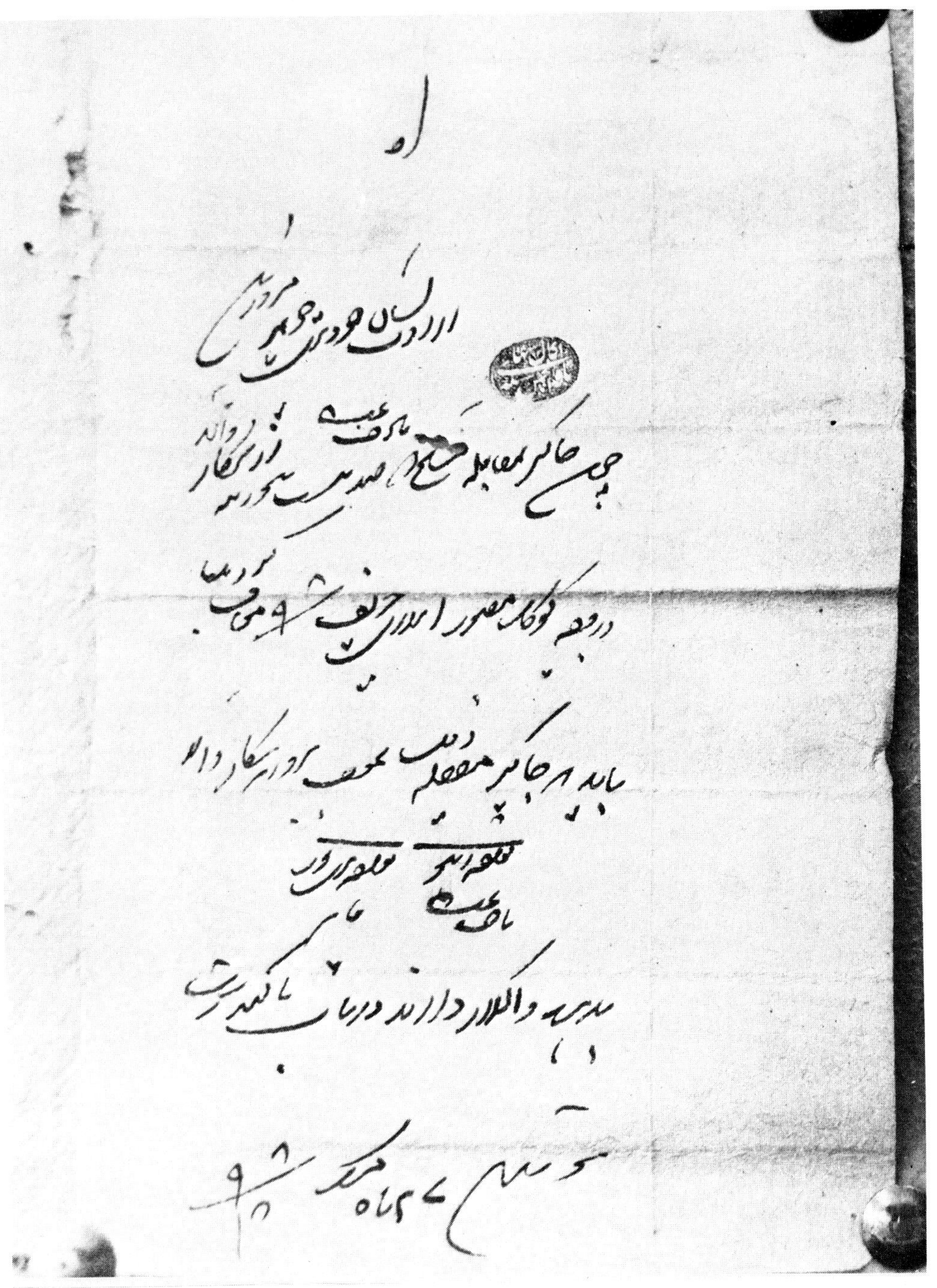

IX : 19,5 x 12,5

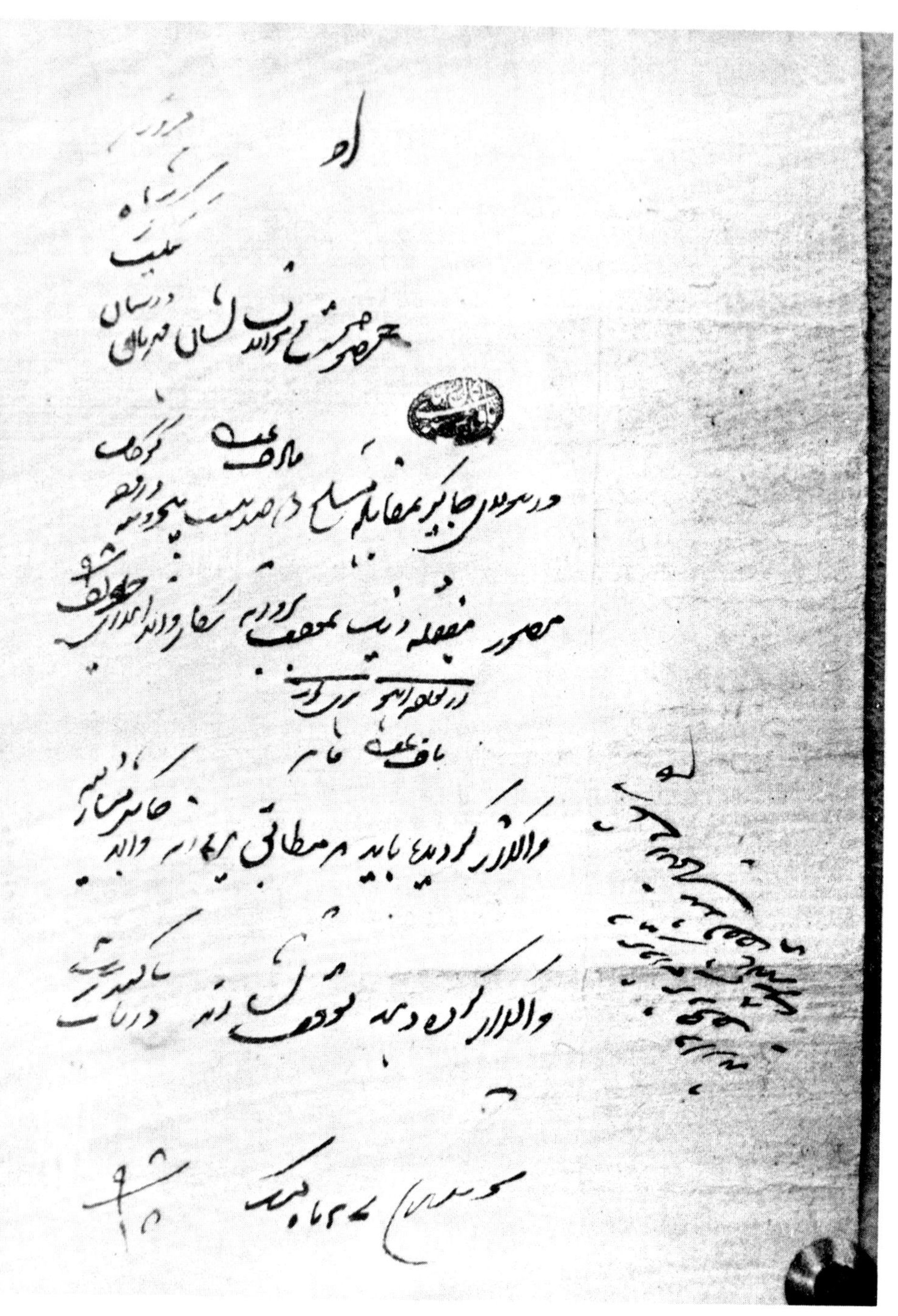

X : 18,5 x 12,5

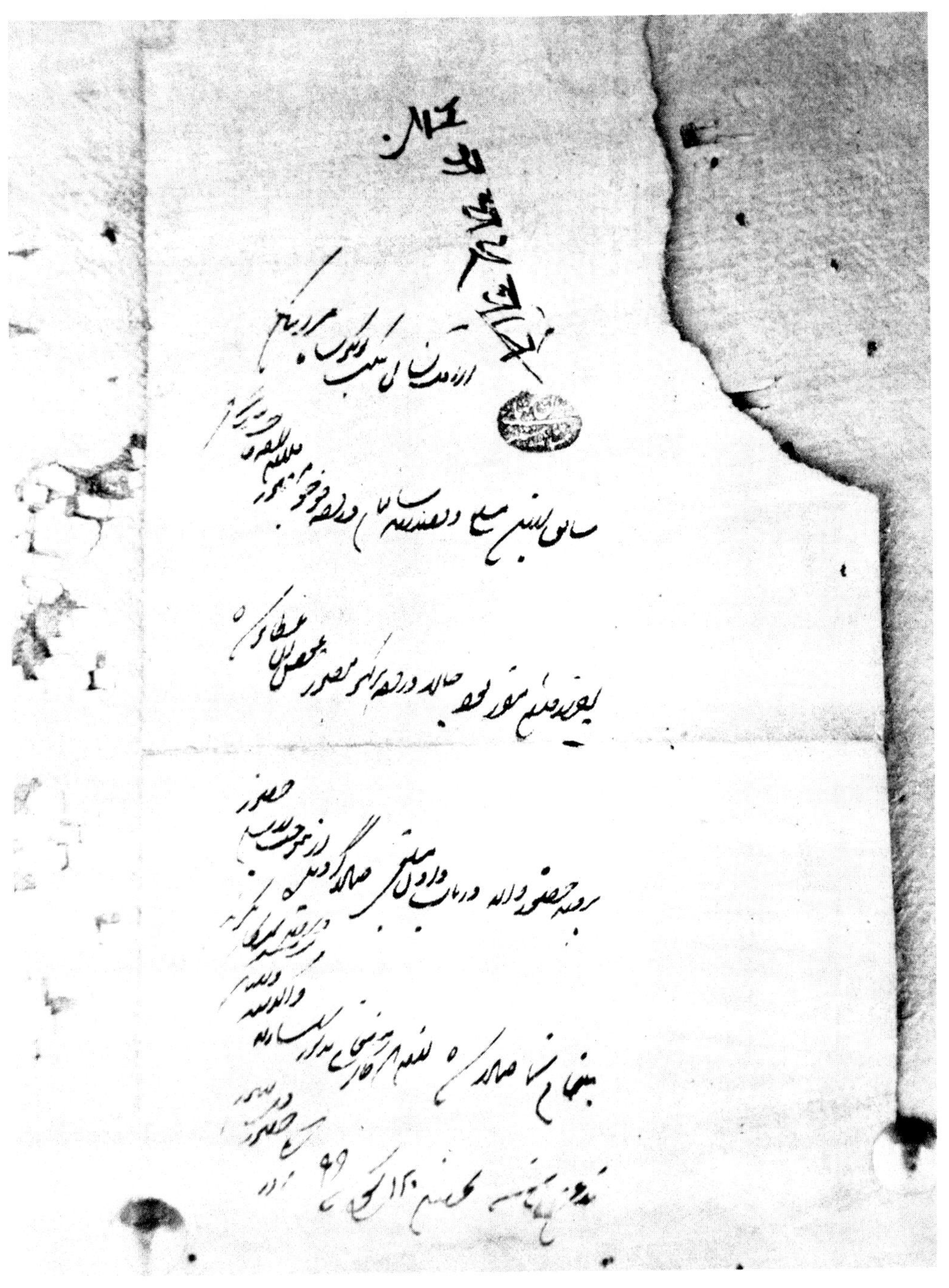

XI : 22 x 12

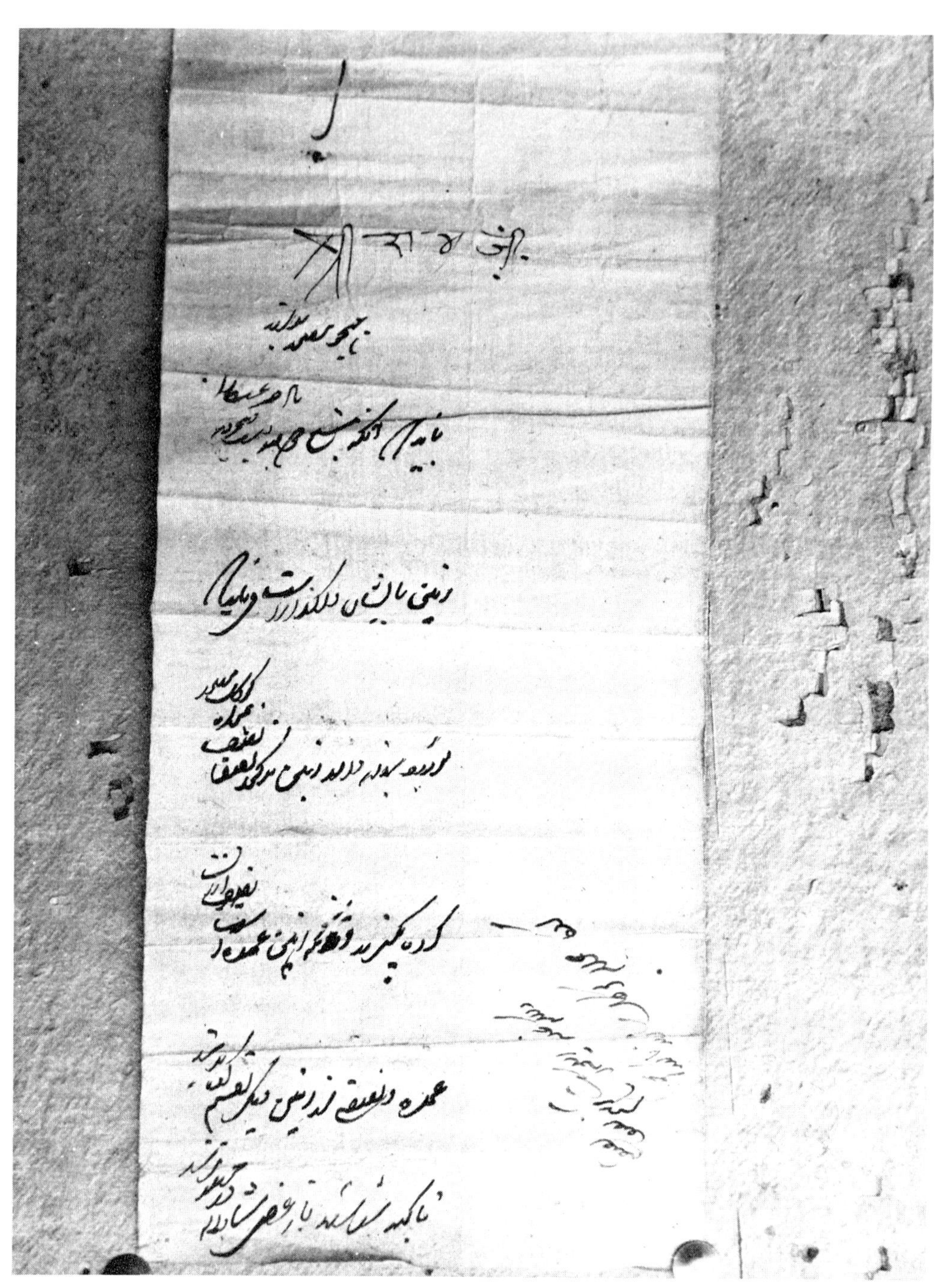

XII : 32 x 14 .

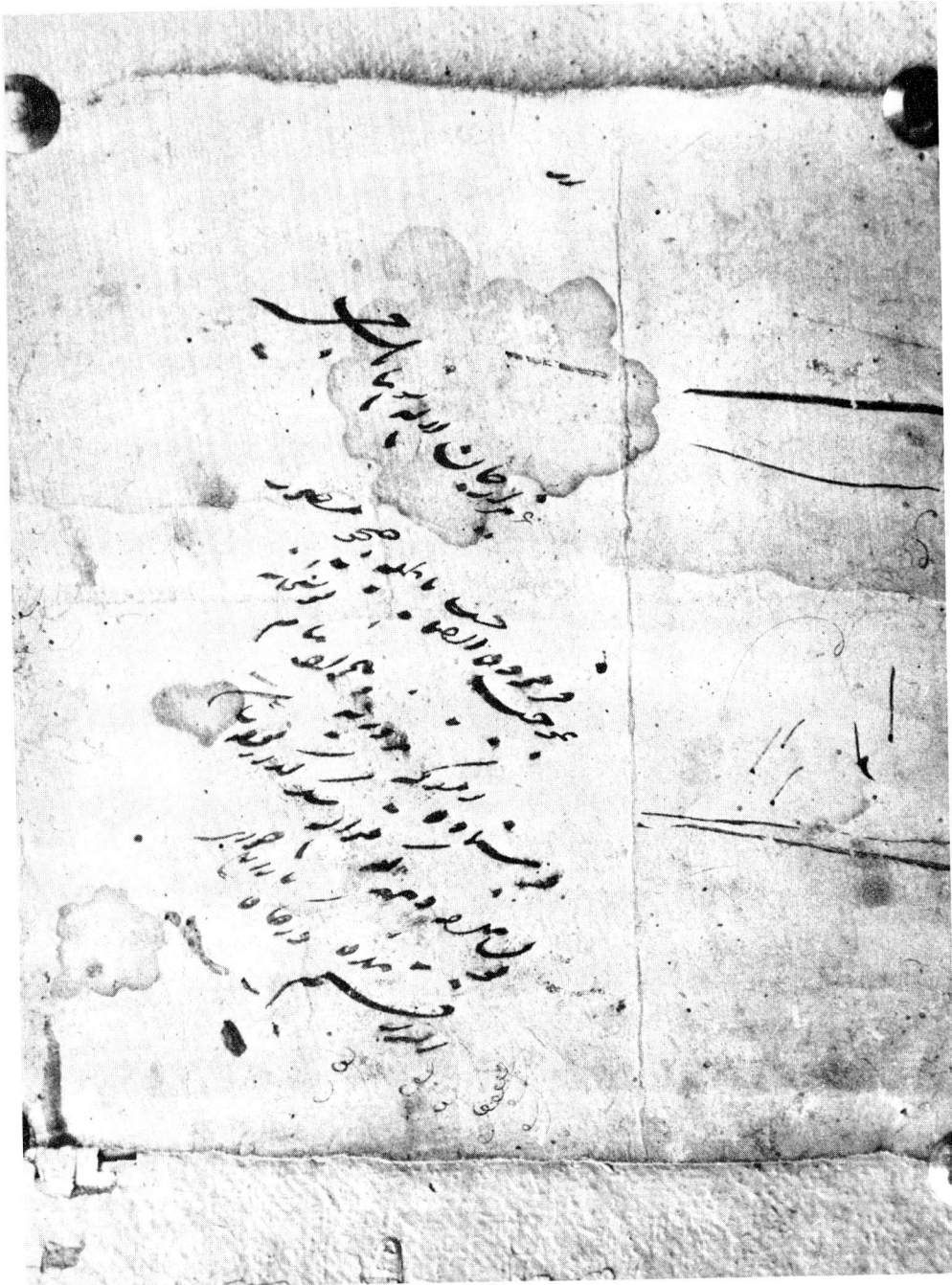

XIII : 16,5 x 15

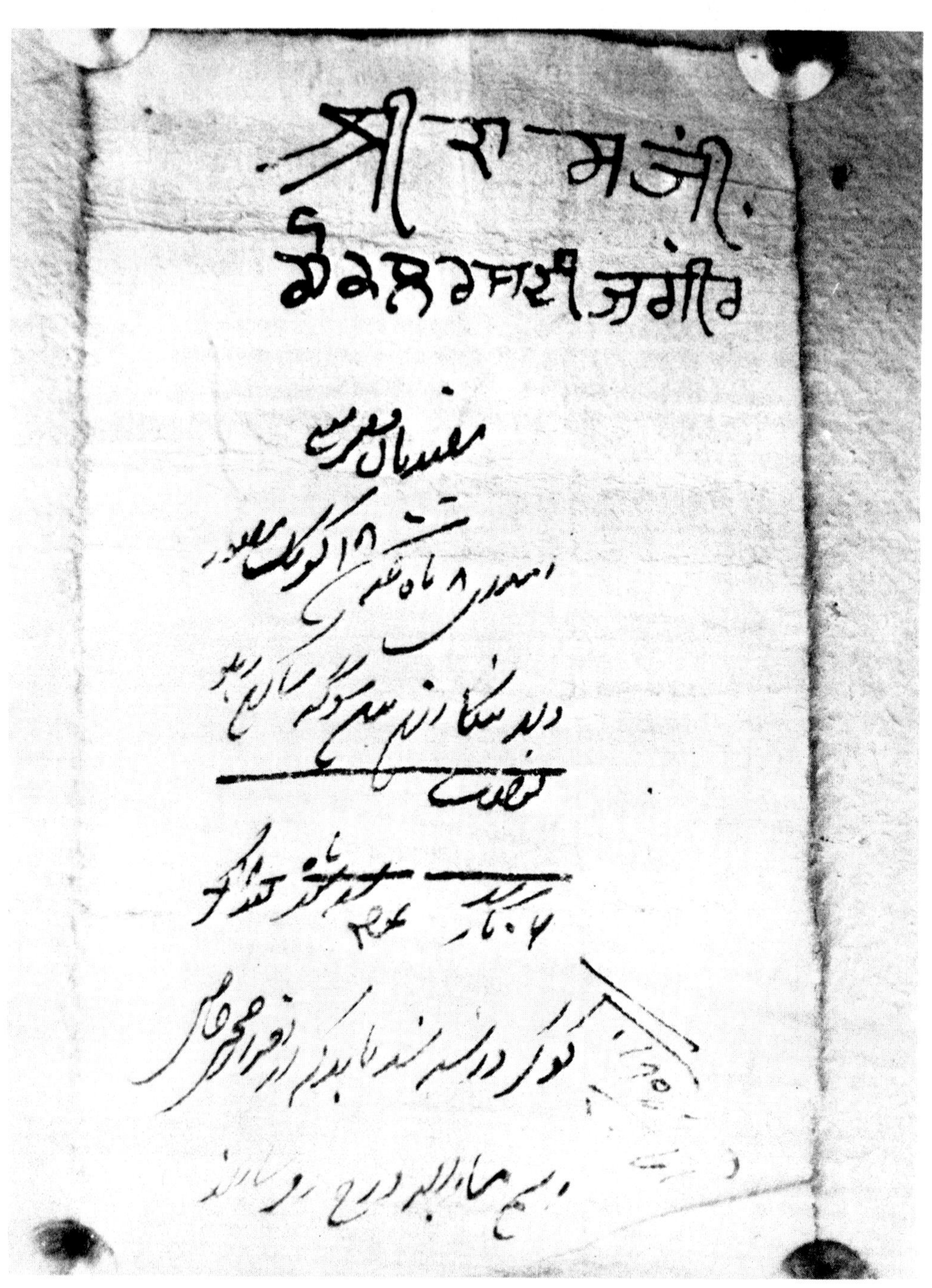

XIV : 14 x 8

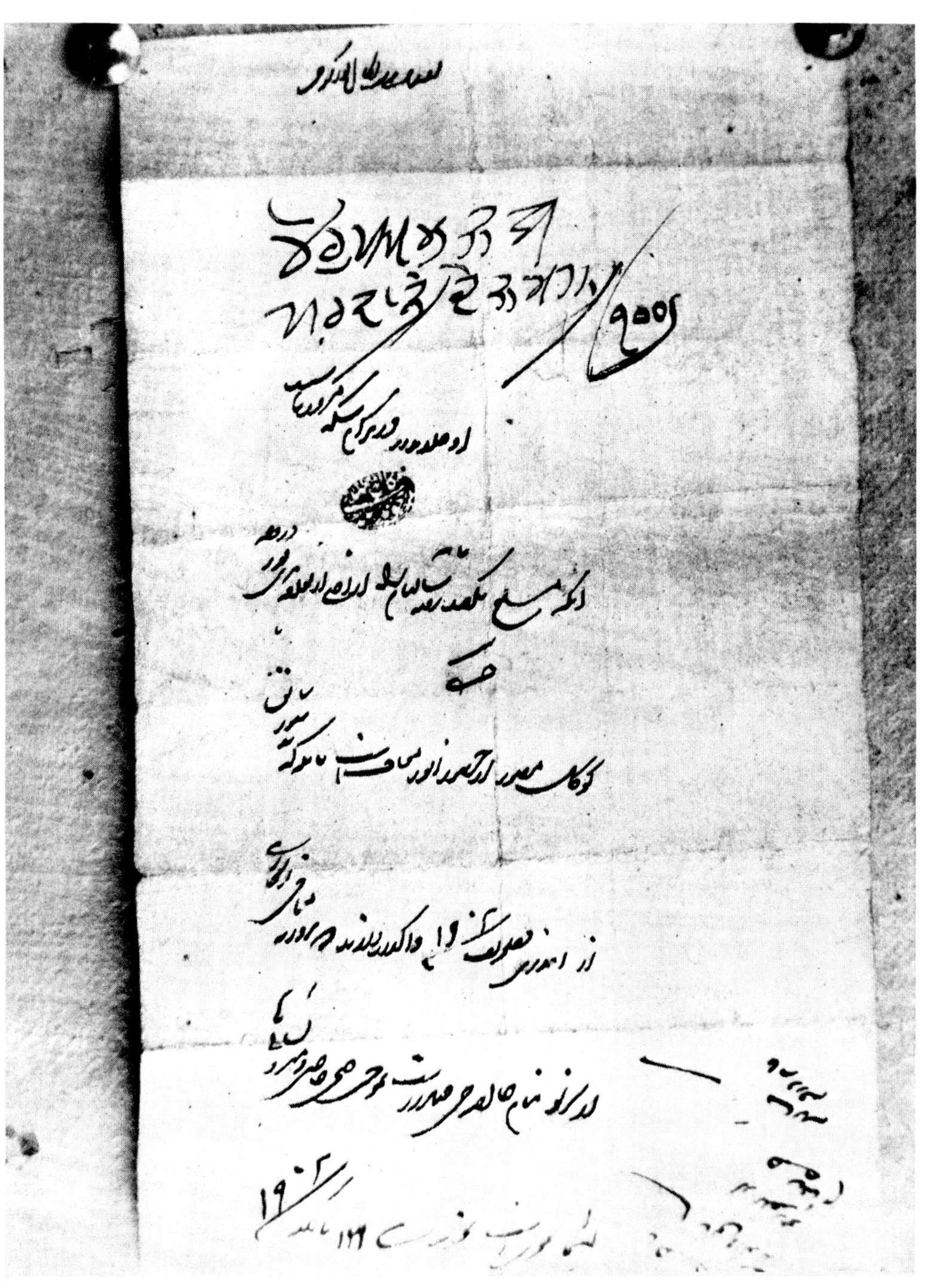

XV : 23,5 x 13

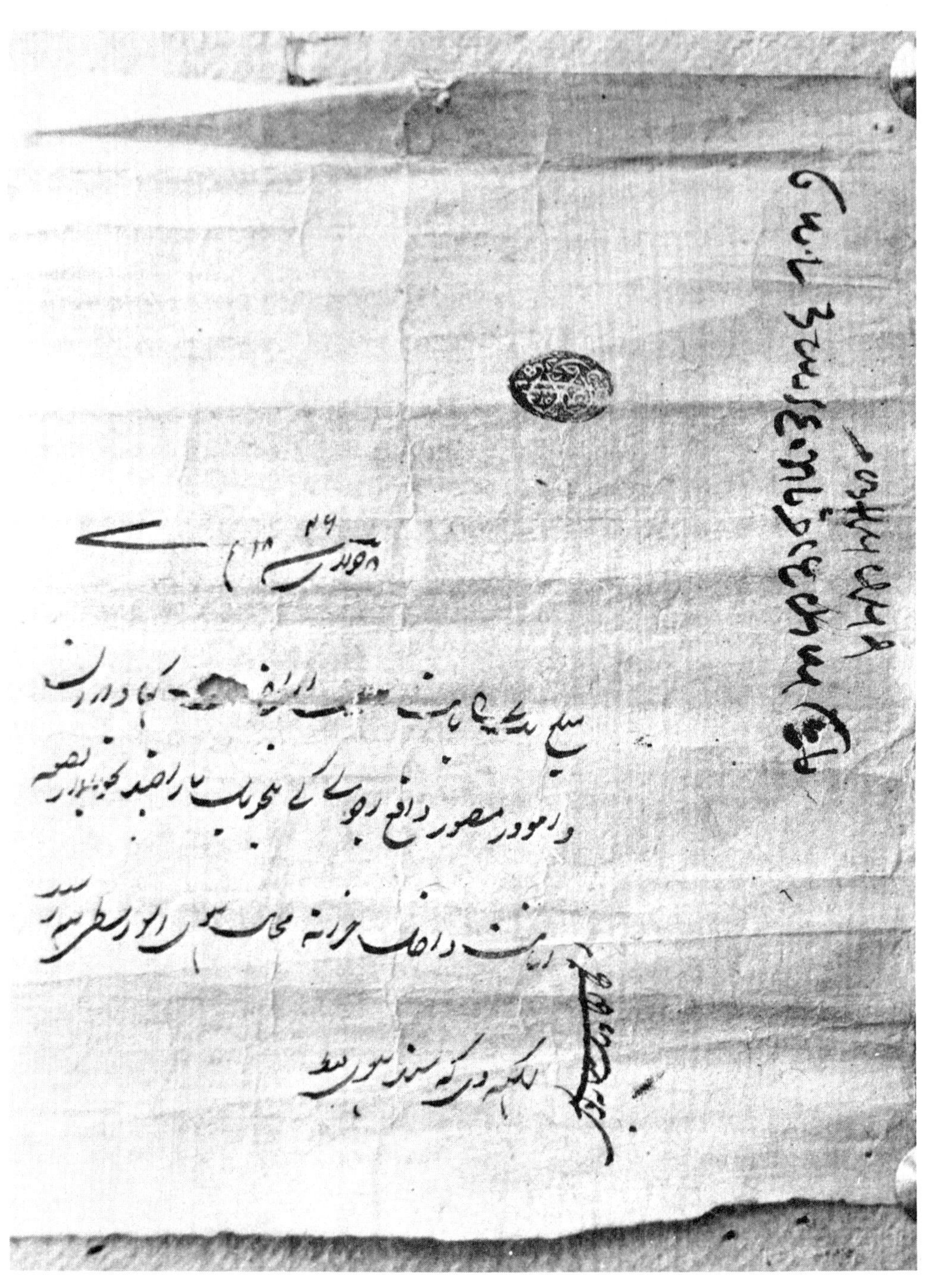

XVI : 17 x 15

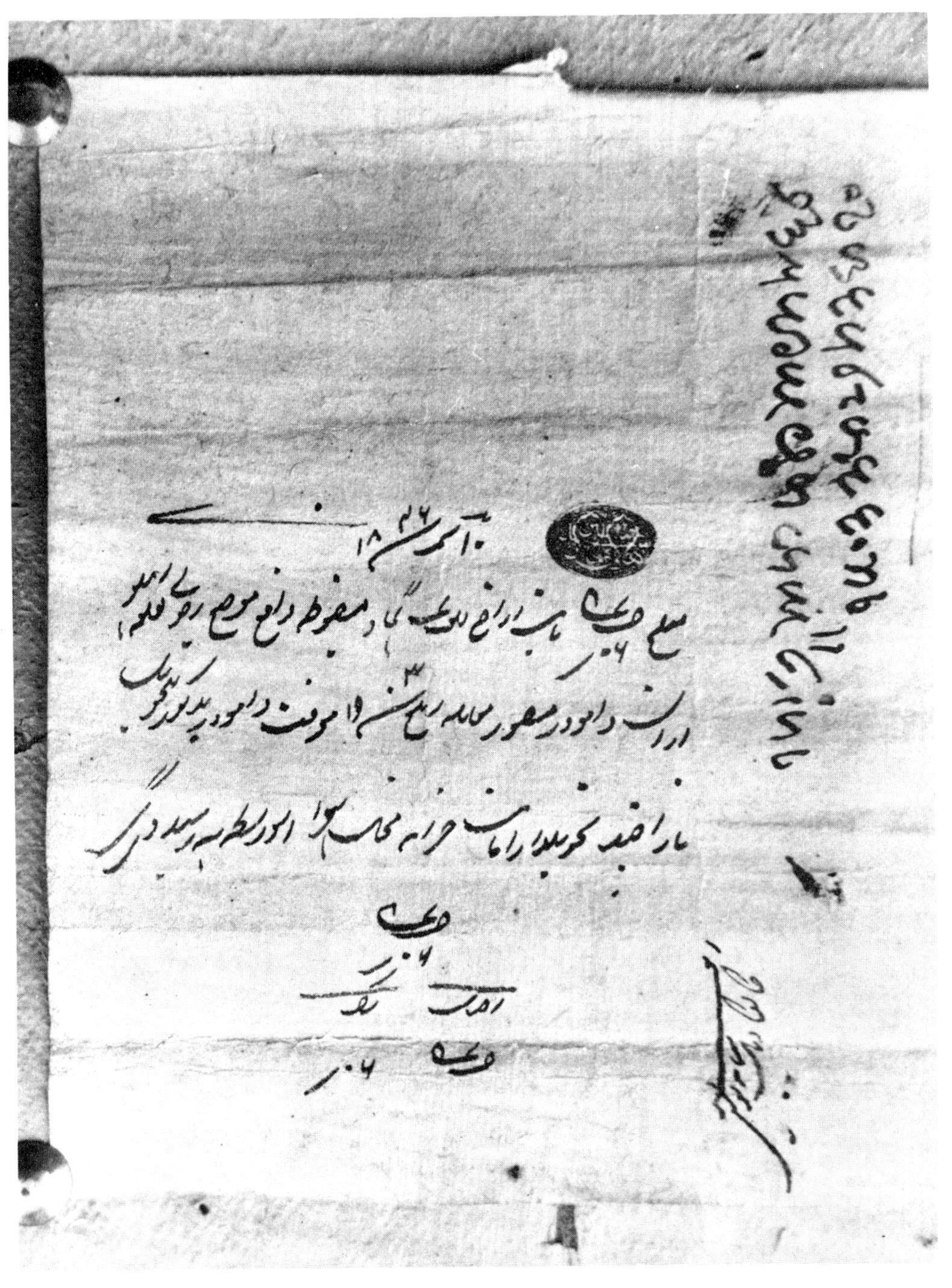

XVII : 16 x 14,5

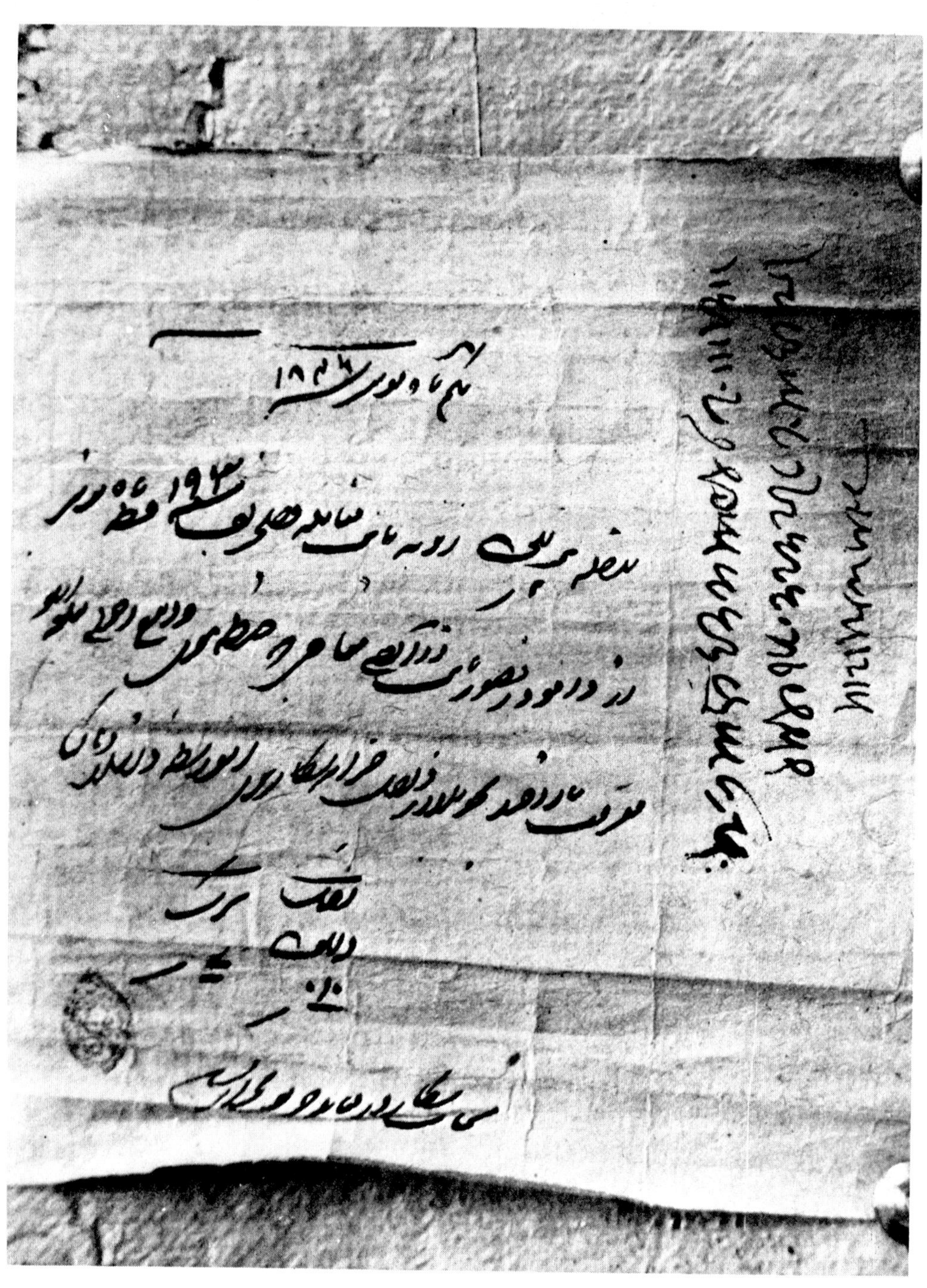

XVIII : 15 x 14,5

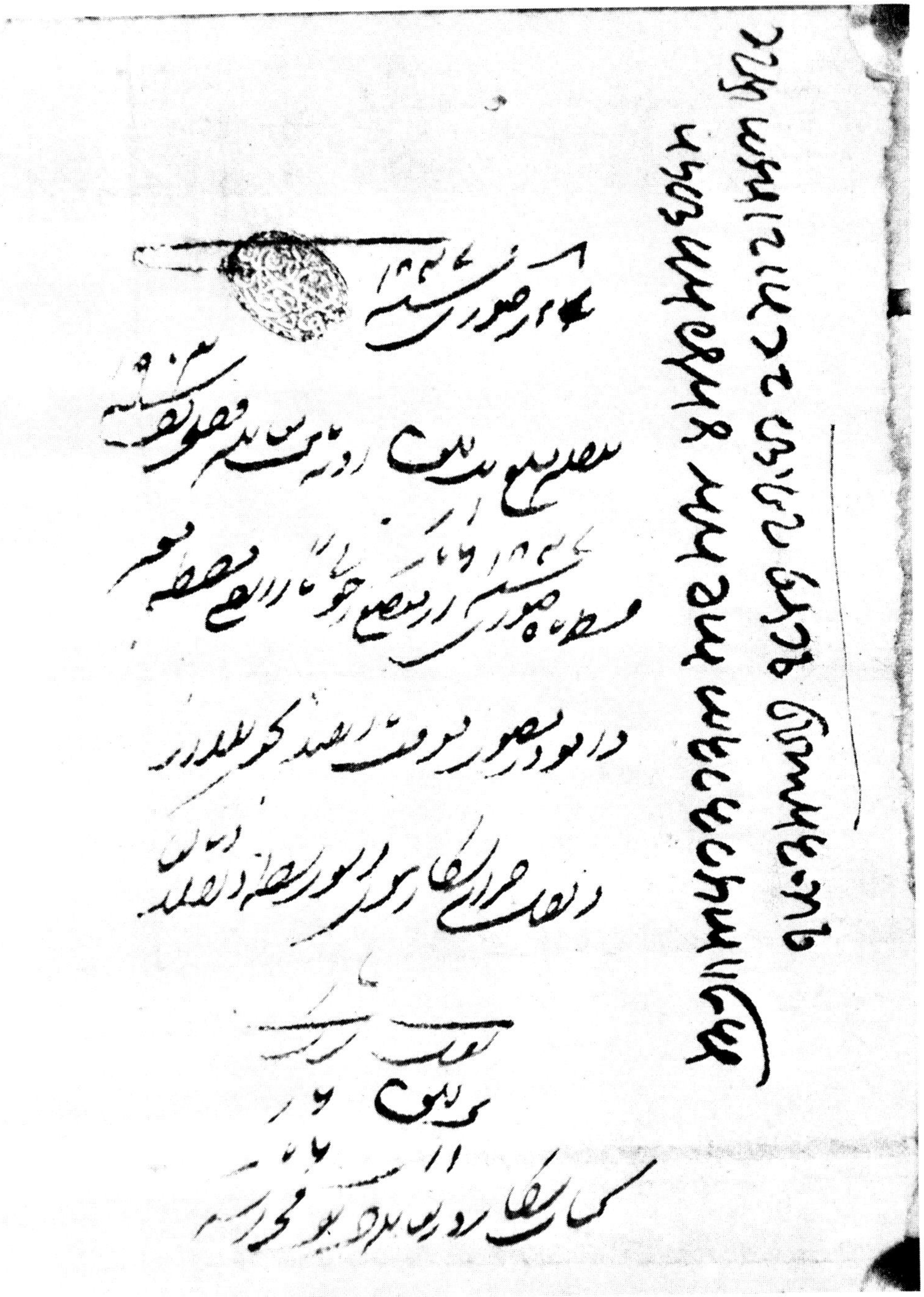

XIX : 14,5 x 11,5

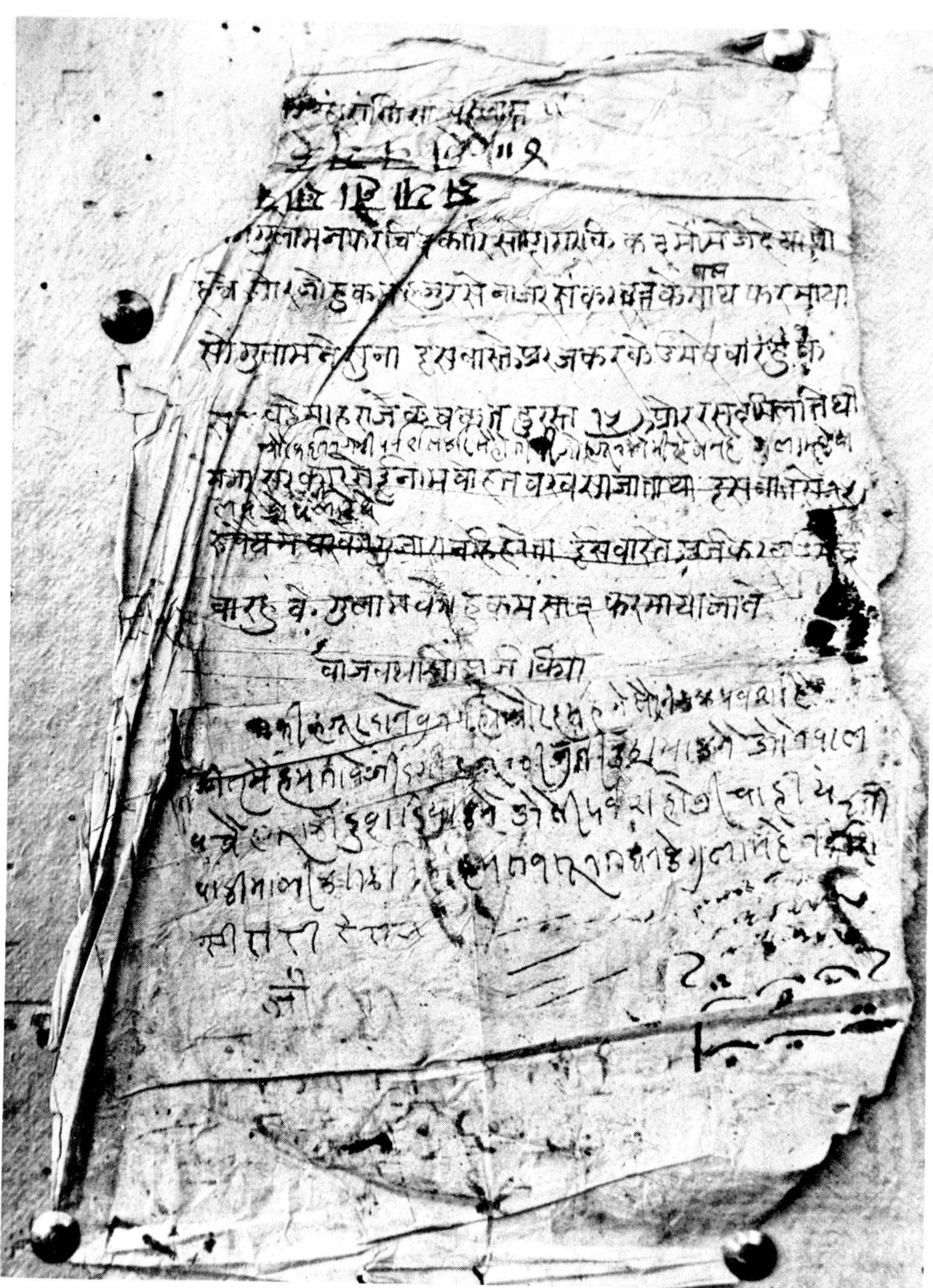

XX : 32 x 2o